CAMBRIDGE LIBRARY COLLECTION

Books of enduring scholarly value

Women's Writing

The later twentieth century saw a huge wave of academic interest in women's writing, which led to the rediscovery of neglected works from a wide range of genres, periods and languages. Many books that were immensely popular and influential in their own day are now studied again, both for their own sake and for what they reveal about the social, political and cultural conditions of their time. A pioneering resource in this area is Orlando: Women's Writing in the British Isles from the Beginnings to the Present (http://orlando.cambridge.org), which provides entries on authors' lives and writing careers, contextual material, timelines, sets of internal links, and bibliographies. Its editors have made a major contribution to the selection of the works reissued in this series within the Cambridge Library Collection, which focuses on non-fiction publications by women on a wide range of subjects from astronomy to biography, music to political economy, and education to prison reform.

English Women of Letters

The Irish novelist Julia Kavanagh (1824–1877) published *English Women of Letters* in two volumes in 1862. The work, which formed a pair with *French Women of Letters* (1862), traces the contribution of English women writers, from the seventeenth century to the nineteenth, to the development and formation of the modern novel. Volume 1 contains biographical sketches of five female authors followed by evaluations of their most important works: Aphra Behn (1640–89) and *Oroonoko*; Sarah Fielding (1710–68) and *David Simple*; Madame D'Arblay (1752–1840), also known as Fanny Burney, and *Evelina* and *Cecilia*; Charlotte Smith (1749–1806) and *Emmeline, Ethelinda* and *The Old Manor House*; and Ann Radcliffe (1764–1823), and four of her gothic novels. This work drew to the attention of the Victorians the importance of these writers, and has served for many generations of English literature students as a biographical companion to women writers. For more information on this author, see http://orlando.cambridge.org/public/svPeople?person_id=kavaju

T0382359

Cambridge University Press has long been a pioneer in the reissuing of out-of-print titles from its own backlist, producing digital reprints of books that are still sought after by scholars and students but could not be reprinted economically using traditional technology. The Cambridge Library Collection extends this activity to a wider range of books which are still of importance to researchers and professionals, either for the source material they contain, or as landmarks in the history of their academic discipline.

Drawing from the world-renowned collections in the Cambridge University Library, and guided by the advice of experts in each subject area, Cambridge University Press is using state-of-the-art scanning machines in its own Printing House to capture the content of each book selected for inclusion. The files are processed to give a consistently clear, crisp image, and the books finished to the high quality standard for which the Press is recognised around the world. The latest print-on-demand technology ensures that the books will remain available indefinitely, and that orders for single or multiple copies can quickly be supplied.

The Cambridge Library Collection will bring back to life books of enduring scholarly value (including out-of-copyright works originally issued by other publishers) across a wide range of disciplines in the humanities and social sciences and in science and technology.

English Women of Letters

of Letters

Biographical Sketches

VOLUME 1

JULIA KAVANAGH

CAMBRIDGE
UNIVERSITY PRESS

CAMBRIDGE UNIVERSITY PRESS

Cambridge, New York, Melbourne, Madrid, Cape Town, Singapore,
São Paolo, Delhi, Dubai, Tokyo

Published in the United States of America by Cambridge University Press, New York

www.cambridge.org
Information on this title: www.cambridge.org/9781108020534

© in this compilation Cambridge University Press 2010

This edition first published 1863
This digitally printed version 2010

ISBN 978-1-108-02053-4 Paperback

The original edition of this book contains a number of colour plates, which cannot
be printed cost-effectively in the current state of technology. The colour scans
will, however, be incorporated in the online version of this reissue, and in printed
copies when this becomes feasible while maintaining affordable prices.

Additional resources for this publication at www.cambridge.org/9781108020534

ENGLISH WOMEN OF LETTERS:

BIOGRAPHICAL SKETCHES.

BY

JULIA KAVANAGH,

AUTHOR OF

"FRENCH WOMEN OF LETTERS,"

"NATHÁLIE," "ADELE,"

&c., &c.

IN TWO VOLUMES.

VOL. I.

LONDON:
HURST AND BLACKETT, PUBLISHERS,
SUCCESSORS TO HENRY COLBURN,
13, GREAT MARLBOROUGH STREET.
1863.

TO THE READER.

THE explanatory preface which was given
with " French Women of Letters " applies
to " English Women of Letters " as well.
Both are parts of one whole, conceived and
written at the same time, and with the
same object—namely, " to show how far,
for the last two centuries and more, women
have contributed to the formation of the
modern novel in the two great literatures
of modern times—the French and the
English."

I will not trouble my readers by repeat‑
ing what I already said at some length on
this subject, but I will remind them of
what may have escaped their memory—
that this selection includes none but long
dead novelists, or amongst the recently
departed, such as have already stood the
test of all merit—time.

CONTENTS OF VOL. I.

ENGLISH WOMEN OF LETTERS.

CHAPTER I.

APHRA BEHN.

Two great literatures have ruled Europe for the last two hundred years: the French and the English. They ruled alone, until, dazzling the world with a delicate and noble genius, long unsuspected, Germany awoke from her slumbers, and poured forth, in a few years, the accumulated treasures of centuries. But even though their sway is no longer undivided, the broad, original line remains; and whatever work of modern literature we open—poem, novel, or history—we find that its spirit is either French or English, or a mingling of both. It may have been modified by Germany or

Spain, by metaphysical subtlety or by epic ballad; but the great original distinction is too clearly impressed to be mistaken by any save the careless.

This is especially true of fiction. Acute critics have traced back the modern novel to purely Teutonic sources; others have sought for it in the broad stream of the Middle Ages, in the romances of chivalry; but that result of many influences with which we began, the Scudéry novel, owed little to the German element, and not much to the heroic romance: it was French, and the manifestation of a new subtle spirit of analysis, *finesse*, and truth. Mighty deeds, strong passions, were fading away; and it is when external life has less hold on attention, when these passions depart, that observation awakens; the less food it has the keener it grows. The Scudéry novel kept some of the grand old forms; the endless loves, the princely heroines, the magnanimous heroes, but it was essentially the fruit of a new school—of a school potent to this day, more potent than ever, spite all its changes. Subtlety, wit, passion, and eloquence have alternately been the French representation of human life—of satire we do not speak, it does not even pretend to be truth—and these qualities have been accompanied by an immense power of impulse and sympathy.

The French novel has always been, and, until the decay of French literature, it promises to be, the most popular of any written. It generalises and appeals best to the feelings and tastes of foreigners. It has been abused and often hated, but it has always been read. Few can resist its attraction, for it has the art of not wearying; its rule, however, is subject to the vicissitudes of great and sudden popularity—it is brief. French novels die quickly, in France and out of it; often when they survive they owe their durability to some extraneous gift—to the fame, the style, the genius of the writer — rarely to the pleasure of the reader.

In English literature it is not so; there, the novel that has ceased to please has ceased to live. English novels have seldom the sudden and universal success of the French, but their power, if less fascinating, is far more durable. They take their stand on safer and less imaginative ground. They do not seem written to propagate certain doctrines, to excite and amuse, but to be true—and truth has an immortal charm. It is surprising to see how lasting an impression they have left in all foreign literature. Wherever we turn we see their trace in form or substance. They have many deficiencies, some of which are painful; they are not, as a rule, great literary works, models of thought or style; they do not always possess the attractions of universal genius or of famous names, but their power is complete; and from the days of Aphra Behn to this, a narrow but stubborn and prevailing strength has been their lot.

The character of the English novel has, for the last seventy years, been much modified by what threatens to become an overwhelming influence—that of women. It has lost its repelling coarseness—a great gain—but it is to be feared that its manliness and its truth are in peril. English novel-writing has well nigh fallen *en quenouille*—for great pictures of human life cannot be called novels. The mere novel, the plain tale, with its limited characters and incidents, is now rarely written by men; their genius takes another bent, and seeks other paths—and it is this that has gained and suffered from feminine influence.

Delicacy it has acquired. Women have certainly not surpassed men in vigorous conception

or portraiture of character, in construction of
story or variety of incident, but they have gone far
beyond them in the feminine attributes of delicacy,
tenderness, and purity. Delicacy, both natural
and acquired, has especially been their gift. The
laws of society have given women a marvellous
faculty for implying that which cannot be told; this
refinement is a part of delicacy and good-breeding,
and is excellent until it prevents truth. It must
not give us a world too sweet, too fair, too good.
The modern English novel is a selection in which
we see the flowers of domestic society; and so
pleased has society grown with this flattered portrait that it will tolerate none other. Fiction must
be pleasant; immorality herself dare not wear her
real mien in its pages; she takes a hard, a cruel
aspect, and loses her indecorous freedom. Worse
still: loves, feelings, enthusiasms, such as no one
ever saw, are to be accepted as possible realities.
The wonderful and often humiliating, but at least
human, contradictions of biography are set aside
to make way for imaginary excellence—imaginary,
yet given as true. This is surely a doubtful good.
Let fiction teach noble lessons, let it avoid debasing
coarseness, let it shew human greatness and virtue;

but neither in good nor in evil let it belie truth, if
it wishes to live.

These strictures, whether just or not, will not,
at least, apply to the woman who opens this line
of English novelists. Too much delicacy or refinement was not the sin of poor Aphra Behn,
or of the times when she wrote.

A letter addressed by a lady to the *Spectator*,
and which appeared in one of its early numbers,
induced Sir Richard Steele to write a paper,
much needed, on the coarseness and indelicacy of
the English stage. Though this unknown corre-
spondent complained to himself of one of his own
plays, he had the good sense and the good feeling
to acquiesce in the justice of her remarks, and to
expunge the passage which had offended her
modesty. But as he had by no means been a
solitary sinner in that respect, as some of his
predecessors had gone far beyond him, and as
amongst the offenders there were two women—
Mrs. Mary Pix and Mrs. Aphra Behn—he did
not lose the opportunity of bestowing upon both
a severe, though merited, reproof.

Mrs. Aphra Behn was a novelist as well as a
dramatist. She was so unfortunate as to deserve

Sir Richard Steele's censure in both characters, and what we know of her, though suggestive of an entertaining life, which we have no right to pronounce actually vicious, is not, however, of a nature to raise either esteem or affection. The inveterate coarseness of her mind sullied Aphra Behn's noblest gifts; beauty, sincerity, wit, an eloquent tongue and a ready pen, perished in that wreck of all that is delicate and refined in woman.

Aphra Johnson, "a gentlewoman by birth, of a good family in the city of Canterbury," was born in that town towards the close of Charles the First's reign. Amongst her father's relatives was Lord Willoughby, who had him appointed Lieutenant-General of Surinam and thirty-six islands besides. Aphra was scarcely beyond the years of infancy when Mr. Johnson and his family embarked for their future home, but we are already told of her accomplishments, amongst which numbered the gift of writing "the prettiest soft, engaging verses in the world;" and as "she was mistress of uncommon charms of body, as well as mind," we are bound to believe in the broken hearts of the lovers this precocious wit and beauty left behind her.

Mr. Johnson never saw the land he had hoped
to rule. He died at sea, but his widow and family
reached Surinam safely. Aphra Behn's description of this luxuriant country is remarkable ; in
this, and in the forcible portraiture of character, lay
her strength, and that of the future English school
of fiction which she not unworthily opened.
There is careless and picturesque power in this
account of a tropical region :—

"It affords all things, both for beauty and use ;
'tis there eternal spring, always the very months of
April, May, and June ; the shades are perpetual,
the trees bearing at once all degrees of leaves and
fruits, from blooming buds to ripe autumn ;
groves of oranges, lemons, citrons, figs, nutmegs,
and noble aromatics continually bearing their
fragrancies ; the trees appearing all like nosegays
adorned with flowers of different kinds ; some are
all white, some purple, some scarlet, some blue,
some yellow—bearing at the same time ripe fruit,
and blooming young, or producing every day new.
The very wood of all these trees has an intrinsic
value above common timber ; for they are, when
cut, of different colours, glorious to behold, and
bear a price considerable to inlay withal. Besides

this, they yield rich balm and gums, so that we
make our candles of such an aromatic substance
as does not only give a sufficient light, but, as
they burn, they cast their perfume all about. Ce-
dar is the common firing, and all the houses are
built with it."

No less vivid and pleasing is her account of her
first home in Surinam :—

"As soon as I came into the country, the best
house in it was presented to me, called Saint
John's Hill. It stood on a vast rock of white
marble, at the foot of which the river ran, a vast
depth down, and not to be descended on that side;
the little waves, still dashing and washing the
foot of this rock, made the softest murmurs and
purlings in the world, and vast quantities of different flowers, eternally blooming, and every day
and hour new, fenced behind them with lofty trees
of a thousand rare forms and colours, that the
prospect was the most ravishing that sands can
create. On the edge of this white rock, towards
the river, was a walk or grove of orange and
lemon trees, about half the length of the Mall
here, whose flowery and fruit-bearing branches
met at the top, and hindered the sun, whose rays

are very fierce there, from entering a beam into
the grove; and the cool air that came from the
river, made it not only fit to entertain people in at
all the hottest hours of the day, but refresh the
sweet blossoms, and made it always sweet and
charming; and sure the whole globe of the world
cannot show so delightful a place as this grove
was; not all the gardens of boasted Italy can
produce a shade so entire as this, which nature
had joined with art to render so exceeding fine;
and 'tis a marvel to see how such vast trees—as
big as English oaks—could take footing on so
solid a rock, and in so little earth as covered that
rock. But all things by nature there are rare,
delightful, and wonderful. But to our sports."

These sports were of the fiercest and most dangerous kind, and give us the dark, terrible aspect of
this land of orange and lemon groves, which
pleased Aphra so well. To search for young
tigers in their dens, to fly for life before the enraged dams, was the amusement in which the
reckless girl took part. She went out on foot in
the morning with women as careless of danger as
herself, and with Europeans whose presence was
no safeguard against the fury of a robbed tigress.

A young black slave, named Cæsar by the English, but Oroonoko and a prince in his own land, accompanied the hunters, and by his daring and his
coolness often delivered them from imminent
peril. Once, as Aphra says, " our heels had not
saved our lives," from the savage might of the
enraged tigress, if, laying down her cub, he had
not met " this monstrous beast of mighty size and
vast limbs," and pierced her ere she sprang.

But Surinam, with its delights and its terrors,
was not destined to be Miss Johnson's home. By
the first opportunity, both she and her mother
returned to England, where she had the honour
of an interview with Charles II., " that wonderful
good-natured and well-bred gentleman," as she
afterwards called him in one of her tales. She at
least possessed all the qualifications that were
calculated to please the king. She was a handsome dark girl, with a clear forehead, fine eyes,
a full and merry mouth, an animated though
voluptuous countenance, and a quick and ready
tongue. She charmed the king by the account
she gave him of Surinam, and moved him to pity
by the tragic history of Prince Oroonoko, which
he desired her to give to the public. She obeyed,

and this, her first novel, had the greatest success.

It was about this time that Aphra Johnson became the wife of Mr. Behn, a London merchant, of Dutch extraction, of whom we know nothing. In 1666, being already a widow, Mrs. Behn was sent to Antwerp by the king, who had conceived no mean opinion of her abilities. England and Holland were not good friends just then, and her mission was diplomatic. Aphra Behn was to watch and report. She watched to some purpose, and curious and interesting, if we knew it all, would be the history of her business and negotiations. What we do know is significant enough. Amongst the merchants of Utrecht was one named Van der Albert, who had seen and loved her in England before the war, and whilst her husband still lived, and who knew the secrets of his country. On him, and the weakness of his passions, she counted for intelligence, and it was to be nearer to him that she made Antwerp her residence. On learning her arrival there, Van der Albert hastened to meet her; he renewed his suit, and was listened to with some favour; a bargain was struck—Aphra Behn was to be his reward, and treason the price he had to pay for her.

So faithfully did he keep his word, that having
appointed an interview with her, by special mes-
senger, he took a long journey to hold with her a
few minutes' conversation, during which he informed her that De Witt and Ruyter were to sail up
the Thames and destroy the English ships in their
harbours. So clear and positive was his information, that, unable to doubt it, she had scarcely
patience to wait his departure till she sent off her
despatches to England.

But if all that Van der Albert had told her was
true, there were traitors in the councils of the
English king, as well as in those of the States of
Holland. And the perjured ministers who could
abet a scheme meant for the ruin and the shame of
their country, and the fools who in all times are
trusted with the weightiest human affairs, now
combined—these because of their folly, the others
because of their infamy—to deride the knowledge
thus received. Mrs. Behn's letter was shown,
laughed at, and made a jest of; her very friends
heard of it and wrote to her to drop politics and
negotiations, and to give them the love scandal of
Antwerp, her own or any other lady's, just as she
pleased; but to let state business rest. The kind

insolence of the advice stung her as her very
denial shows in this passage of her reply to a
friend :—

"Your remarks upon my politick capacity, though
they are sharp, touch me not, but recoil on those
that have not made use of the advantages they
might have drawn from thence ; and are doubly
to blame — first, in sending a person in whose
ability, sense, and veracity they could not confide ;
and next, not to understand when a person indifferent tells them a probable story, and which, if
it came to pass, would sufficiently punish their in-
credulity ; and which, if followed, would have put
them on their guard against a vigilant and indus-
trious foe, who watched every opportunity of
returning the several repulses and damages they
had met with of late from them . . . But I
have let these idle reflections (for such must all be
that regard our wretched statesmen) divert me
from a more agreeable relation.   To comply,
therefore, with your request in its full extent, I
shall give you an account of both my own adventures, and those of a lady of my acquaintance ;
and with her I'll begin, for 'tis but civil to give
place to a stranger."

Then follows the story of Lucilla, which reads very much like an extra novel, and not a good one, of Mrs. Behn's. The account she gives of her Dutch lovers in another letter has a greater air of truth, and is at least more entertaining:—

"Dear Friend,—Though our courtiers will not allow me to do any great matters with my politics, I am sure you must grant that I have done so with my eyes, when I shall tell you I have made two Dutchmen in love with me. Dutchmen, do you mind me, that have no soul for anything but gain; that have no pleasure or interest but the bottle. . . . Yet I, sir, this very numerical person your friend and humble servant, have set two of them in a blaze; two of very different ages (I was going to say degrees, sir, but I remember there are no degrees in Holland). Van der Albert is about thirty-two, of a hale constitution, something more sprightly than the rest of his countrymen; and though infinitely fond of his interest and an irreconcilable enemy to Monarchy, has by the force of love been obliged to let me into some secrets that might have done our King, and, if not our court, our country, no small service. But I shall say no more of this lover till I see you, for some particular reasons which you shall then likewise know. My other is about twice his age, nay, and bulk too, though Albert be not the most Barbary shape you have seen; you must know him by the name of Van Bruin. . . . He had not visited me often before I began to be sensible of the influence of my eyes on this old piece of worm-eaten touchwood, but he had not the confidence (and that's much) to tell me he loved me; and modesty, you know, is no common fault of his countrymen, though I rather impute it to a love of himself, that he would not run the hazard of being turned into ridicule in so disproportionate a declaration. He often insinuated that he knew a man of wealth and substance, though stricken, indeed, in years, and on that account not so agreeable as a younger man, that was passionately in love with me, and desired to know whether my heart was so far engaged that his friend should not entertain any hopes."

The fair Aphra declined giving an aged lover any encouragement, spite of which assurance he wrote to her a long letter, which, as she had the name of a wit, he worded in a strange style, of which the following sample will suffice :—

" Most transcendant charmer,—I have strove
often to tell you the tempests of my heart, and
with my own mouth scale the walls of your affections; but, terrified with the strength of your
fortifications, I concluded to make more regular
approaches, and first attack you at a farther distance, and try first what a bombardment of letters
would do," &c.

Undeterred by this formidable attack, gay Mrs.
Behn replied—

" Extraordinary sir,—I received your extraordinary epistle, which has had extraordinary effects,
I assure you, and was not read without an extraordinary pleasure. I never doubted the zeal of your
countrymen in making new discoveries, in fixing new
trades, in supplanting their neighbours, and in en-
grossing the wealth and traffic of both the Indies;
but, I confess, I never expected so wise a nation
should at last have set out for the island of love." In
this strain, if we are to believe Mrs. Behn—and we
must not be too sure of that—the correspondence
went on, until Van der Albert rid her of poor
Van Bruin, and her own wit of Van der Albert;
for probably conceiving that none need keep faith
with traitors, she consigned him to his wife; soon

after which he died of a fever; and her mission being over, she went back to England, where she henceforth resided.

Henceforth, too, she led a literary life. She wrote for her bread, and wrote much and carelessly. She borrowed from French, Spanish, and English authors. She published three volumes of miscellaneous poems, in which Rochester and Sir George Etherege, among the rest, were her coadjutors. Her poems were bad, though she contributed the paraphrase of " Œnone's Epistle to Paris," in the English translation of " Ovid's Epistles," and received the following handsome compliment from Dryden in the preface to that work :—"I was desired to say that the author, who is of the fair sex, understood not Latin. But if she does not, I am afraid she has given us account to be ashamed who do." Her plays, some of which had great success, were so coarse as to offend even in that coarse age. Her novels were open to the same objection, and were rarely original. Sometimes, but not often, she openly acknowledged her translations, as in the case of La Rochefoucauld's "Maxims," and Fontenelle's " Plurality of Worlds." Towards the close of her life, she included mathematics, philosophy, theology even, in her pursuits, but it must be confessed that she excelled in nothing. Like all persons of lively minds, she took interest in many things; she found pleasure in those " rare flies, of amazing forms and colours," which she brought from Surinam, and presented " to his Majesty's antiquary," and, at a later period, she took amusement in the arid details of chronology, but her versatility was productive of no substantial result.

Of her life as a writer and a woman we do not know much, though it has been related by one who knew her long and well, who loved her truly and defended her warmly, but with more zeal than boldness—for, without venturing to reveal her name, she merely entitled herself " one of the fair sex." But what befell Aphra Behn, till from youth she reached maturity and death, matters little to us now. There is a strange sameness in the course of human action, and variety, infinite and wonderful, in human beings. What Aphra Behn was, we know well. The praise of her friends, the censure of her enemies, her own works, leave us little doubt concerning the nature of one who, what-

c 2

ever her faults were, was, at least, free and open.

Two great passions she seems to have had—the first and mightiest was pleasure; the second, literature. She managed to combine both in an unusual degree. So fond was she of company, that she wrote a good deal of " Oroonoko," and of her other novels, in a roomful of her friends, keeping up her share of the conversation all the time. She had the sociable qualities and attractions, as well as the sociable inclinations. Apart from her beauty, which was of the bold, voluptuous sort, she was of a temper open and generous; quick to resent, but easily appeased. Her wit was sharp, boisterous, and indelicate; for she who could scarcely write ten pages without coarseness, could not be modest in her conversation. Yet her powers of talking were great; we can be sure of that, not merely from the testimony of those who knew her, but from the reckless, good-humoured facility of her style. It is, essentially, the style of a good talker, forcible but careless, and often incorrect. That agreeable gift she only exercised with those whom she called " plain dealers," men and women who, like herself, held pleasure the great aim of

life, and scouted hypocrisy. How far she carried
her maxims, we cannot tell ; her biographer and
friend warmly declares that she never saw aught
in her " unbecoming the just modesty of our sex,
though more gay. and free than the folly of the
precise will allow."

But granting that her life remained pure, which
is possible even in a woman fond of pleasure, surrounded by lovers, and who philosophically said
of religion, "that it would but destroy the tranquillity of the heathen Indians," one thing is certain, pure her mind was not, but tainted to the
very core. She loved grossness for its own sake,
because it was congenial to her. She wrote
dramas which, though not worse than those of her
cotemporaries, revolted the public as proceeding
from a woman, yet, braving censure and reproof,
with an independence worthy a better cause, she
persisted in her course. The noble examples of
Mademoiselle de Scudéry and Madame de la
Fayette were lost upon her—she read their works,
she knew well their object, and she wrote not one
coarse passage the less for either.

True, the reaction on the Puritan severity had
defiled English literature far and wide ; but the

literature of France was not pure when French-
women began to write. To their eternal honour—
and it is an honour which, if it soar not as high,
at least sinks deeper than that of genius, the
women of that country, when they took up a pen,
did their best to ennoble women, and compel men
into delicacy. The disgrace of Aphra Behn and
of her pupils is that, instead of raising man to
woman's moral standard, they sank woman to the
level of man's coarseness. The very men felt it,
and not without justice did they arraign the
offender. Astrea, the divine and the incompara-
ble, as her friends called her—the author of novels,
plays, and poems with plenty of merit in them —
the beauty, the wit, she " who could sooner forgive
an injury than do one," declares her biographer—
the woman who, whatever her faults were, loved
her country, and who, had she been heeded,
would have served it well, got no mercy from
opinion; one error condemned her, even with posterity—her generous pity for the noble slave, Oroonoko, was called guilty love. There was no proof
of this—everything she wrote on the subject con-
tradicted the supposition; but the conclusion was
satisfactory—it was adopted, and it is not entirely

rejected to this day. Of the man whom she did
love, and to whom her adoring love-letters were
addressed, we hear little and know nothing;
scandal, which made itself so busy with remote
Oroonoko, did not trouble itself with this English
Lysander.

She also called him Lycidas, and wrote him letters in which she signed herself Astrea. From
these letters it appears that he was a cold, formal,
and severe man, and probably he had soon
wearied of a love which might flatter his vanity,
but had never much moved his heart. His coldness only added to her ardour. It irritated her to
a sort of frenzy; he made her, as she said, " write
a thousand madnesses," and, without caring for
it, he led her into all the follies which love delights
in. Once, of her own accord, she vowed to see
no man's face between two of his visits, and they
were not frequent; for he could pass by the end
of the street where she lived and go on to the
coffee-house, rather than give his expecting mistress " the greatest pleasure of her life—his dear,
dull, melancholy company." In vain she passionately asked him to show his love, " there being
nothing so grateful to God and mankind as plain

dealing;" in vain she humbly entreated him to pardon "the faults he had created," and indulged herself and tormented him with all the vehemence of "a woman violent in all her passions," as she calls herself, and "who naturally hated all the little arts of her sex."

Lycidas allowed himself to be adored, kept aloof or came seldom, and was so cool that she could ask him to tell her at least the bitter truth; "at least say, my honest friend Astrea, I neither do love thee, nor can, nor ever will; at least, let me say you were generous, and told me plain, blunt truths."

We have no proof that Lycidas took this trouble. Her passion entertained him well enough, and it does not appear that he gave her any serious repulse. But, indeed, we know no more about it than what her letters tell us, and the biographer who published them did not choose to add any information to their context. Who and what Lycidas was we know not; and now that two hundred years have well-nigh gone by, we can let his coldness and her fervour rest in the dust and obscurity of the grave. Hers was made in the cloisters of Westminster Abbey; there, for all we know, she still

rests, beneath a plain black marble slab, inscribed
with her name, the date of her death, the 16th of
April, 1689, and a eulogistic epitaph, in which
occur these two lines:

> "Here lies a proof that wit can be
> Defence enough against mortalitie."

Vain boast! The grave, the name, the poems,
the novels and histories, the plays and dramas, of
Aphra Behn have shared one fate, oblivion. Hers
was one of those lives, and their name is legion,
where the fairest gifts are foolishly cast away. It
bears a lesson and a meaning, but both are sad.

The friend and companion who wrote her life
has given us the history of a strange vision
which the fair Aphra beheld on her return from
Antwerp to England.

"Sir Bernard Gascoign had brought with him
from Italy several admirable telescopes and pro-
spective glasses; and looking through one of them
when the day was very calm and clear, espied
a strange apparition floating on the water, which
was also seen by all in their turn that looked
through it; which made 'em conclude that they
were painted glasses that were put at the ends, on
purpose to surprise and amuse those that look

through them; till after having taken 'em out,
rubbed and put 'em in again, they found the same
thing floating toward the ship, which was now
come so near as to be within view without the
glass. I have often heard her assert that the
whole company saw it. The figure was this :—a
four square floor of various coloured marbles, from
which ascended rows of fluted and twisted pillars,
embossed round with climbing vines and flowers
and waving streamers, that received an easy
motion from the air; upon the pillars a hundred
little Cupids clambered with fluttering wings. This
strange pageant came almost near enough for one
to step out of the ship into it before it vanished;
after which, and a short calm, followed by so
violent a storm, that having driven the ship upon
the coast, she split in sight of land; but the people,
by the help of the inhabitants and boats from the
shore, were all saved; and our Astrea arrived safe
though tired to London, from a voyage that gained
her more reputation than profit."

Not an unapt figure of her life is this vision
which Aphra dreamed or saw. Even thus did her
youth open, a lovely pageant floating on a calm
sea, adorned with flowers and streamers gaily

waving, whilst the fluttering Cupids hovered on rosy wing around its fluted and twisted pillars. But as the vision melted into empty space, and the calm turned into storm and wreck, as the journey ended with more reputation than profit, so did all fade away from the grasp of this gay lover of pleasure. Youth, beauty, love, forsook her; ambition's short day ended in mortification and regret, penury conquered wit, and, glad to escape total ruin, she sank on those obscure shores of literature where she laboured for a living, and waged unprofitable war with her censors, till she reached a grave consecrated by neither honour nor fame.

CHAPTER II.

OROONOKO.

THE novels and histories of Mrs. Behn have long
ceased to be read; the faults of style in which
they all partake, the want of interest of many of
them, are no doubt amongst the motives for which
these tales, though short and told with much
spirit, are wholly neglected. They are also no
longer read, for a very excellent reason, which the
following significant passage from one of Sir
Walter Scott's works of biography shows in the
fairest aspect:—

" The editor was acquainted with an old lady
of family, who assured him that in her younger
days Mrs. Behn's novels were as currently upon
the toilette as the works of Miss Edgeworth at
present; and described with some humour her

own surprise when the book falling into her
hands after a long interval of years, and when its
contents were quite forgotten, she found it impossible to endure at the age of fourscore what at
fifteen she, like all the fashionable world of the
time, had perused without an idea of impropriety."

The public is like the old lady; it has ceased to
read coarse books and will no longer tolerate them,
and those tales of Mrs. Behn's which escape that
reproach are flat and uninteresting. She could
not invent, but she could relate well, spite her
want of grammar. Her way of telling a story
is of the best, for it is that which gives life to the
lightest matter. How lively is this account of a
certain " Prince, young and gloriously attended,
called Prince Tarquin," who appeared in Flanders
during her stay there, and whose adventures form
the groundwork of one of her tales :—

" He was all the discourse of the town; some
laughing at his title, others reverencing it ; some
cried that he was an impostor, others that he had
made his title as plain as if Tarquin had reigned
but a year ago. Some made friendships with
him, others would have nothing to say to him;
but all wondered where his revenue was that sup-

ported this grandeur, and believed that he could make his descent from the Roman kings very well out—but that he could not lay so good a claim to the Roman land. . . . But the men might be of what opinion they pleased concerning him, the ladies were all agreed that he was a prince, and a young handsome prince, and a prince not to be resisted; he had all their wishes, all their eyes, and all their hearts. They now dressed only for him, and what church he graced was sure that day to have the beauties, and all that thought themselves so."

"You may believe our amorous Miranda was not the least conquest he made. She no sooner heard of him, which was as soon as he arrived, but she fell in love with his very name. Jesu! a young King of Rome! Oh! 'twas so novel, that she doated on the title, and had not cared whether the rest had been man or monkey almost."

But though Mrs. Behn could write in this fresh, pleasant vein, though she had a keen eye for truth and knew how to adorn it with lively speech, that inner truth which lies in the faculty called imagination was scarcely known to her. The only one of her tales that, spite all its defects, can still be read with entertainment, is that in which she invented least, and by far the best portions of that story are those that are related as having come under her special observation. Indeed, " Oroonoko " can scarcely be called a novel ; it is a book of travels, and a most picturesque one ; a biography, and one both noble and 'tragic. We may doubt, indeed, the accuracy of some of Mrs. Behn's statements ; we cannot doubt the general truth of this lamentable history, which is told, moreover, with infinite vigour and spirit.

" The King of Coromantien was of himself a man of an hundred and odd years old, and had no son, though he had many beautiful black wives : for most certainly there are beauties that can charm of that colour. In his younger years he had many gallant men too, his sons, thirteen of whom died in battle, conquering when they fell ; and he had only left him, for his successor, one grandchild, son of one of those dead victors, who, as soon as he could bear a bow in his hand and a quiver at his back, was sent into the field to be trained up by one of the oldest generals to war ; where, from his natural inclination to arms and the occasions

given him, with the good conduct of the old general,
he became, at the age of seventeen, one of the most
expert captains and bravest soldiers that ever saw
the field of Mars : so that he was adored as the
wonder of all the world and the darling of the
soldiers. .   .   .   .   .   . At the
finishing of that war, which had continued for two
years, the prince came to court, where he had
hardly been a month together, from the time of his
sixth year to that of seventeen ; and 'twas amazing
to imagine where it was he learned so much humanity, or, to give his accomplishments a juster
name, where 'twas he got that real greatness of
soul, those refined notions of true honour, that absolute generosity, and that softness' that was
capable of the highest passions of love and gallantry, whose objects were almost continually fighting
men, or those mangled or dead, who heard no
sounds but those of war and groans. Some part
of it we may attribute to the care of a Frenchman of wit and learning, who, finding it turn to a
very good account to be a sort of royal tutor to
this young black, and perceiving him very ready,
apt, and quick of apprehension, took a great pleasure to teach him morals, language, and science,

and was for it extremely beloved and valued by him. Another reason was, he loved, when he came from war, to see all the English gentlemen that traded thither ; and did not only learn their language, but that of the Spaniards also, with whom he traded afterwards for slaves.

"I have often seen and conversed with this great man, and been a witness to many of his mighty actions, and do assure my reader the most illustrious courts could not have produced a braver man, both for greatness of courage and mind; a judgment more solid, or wit more quick, and a conversation more quick and diverting. He knew almost as much as if he had read much; he had heard of the late civil wars in England, and the deplorable death of our great monarch, and would discourse of it with all the sense and abhorrence of the injustice imaginable. He had an extreme good and graceful mien, and all the civility of a well-bred, great man. He had nothing of barbarity in his nature, but in all points addressed himself as if his education had been in some European court.

" This great and just character of Oroonoko gave me an extreme curiosity to see him, especially when I knew he spoke French and English, and

that I could talk with him. But though I had
heard so much of him, I was as greatly surprised
when I saw him as if I had heard nothing of him;
so beyond all report I found him. He came into
the room, and addressed himself to me, and some
other women, with the best grace in the world.
He was pretty tall, but of a shape the most exact
that can be fancied—the most famous statuary
could not form the figure of a man more admirably turned from head to foot. His face was
not of that brown, rusty black which most of that
nation are, but of a perfect ebony, or polished
jet. His eyes were the most awful that could be
seen, and very piercing; the white of them being
like snow, as were his teeth. His nose was
rising and Roman, instead of African and flat;
his mouth, the finest-shaped that could be seen—
far from those great turned lips which are so
natural to the rest of the negroes. The whole
proportion and air of his face was so noble and
exactly formed, that, bating his colour, there could
be nothing in nature more beautiful, agreeable,
and handsome. There was no one grace wanting that bears the standard of true beauty. His
hair came down to his shoulders, by the aids of

art, which was by pulling it out with a quill, and
keeping it combed, of which he took particular
care. Nor did the perfections of his mind come
short of those of his person; for his discourse was
admirable upon almost any subject, and whoever
had heard him speak would have been convinced
of their errors, that all fine wit is confined to the
white men, especially to those of Christendom,
and would have confessed that Oroonoko was as
capable even of reigning well, and of governing
as wisely, had as great a soul, as politic maxims,
and was as sensible of power, as any prince civiliz-
ed in the most refined schools of humanity, or
the most illustrious courts.

"This prince, such as I have described him, whose
soul and body were so admirably adorned, was as
capable of love as 'twas possible for a brave and
gallant man to be; and in saying that, I have
named the highest degree of love; for sure great
souls are most capable of that passion."

The love of this romantic black fell on Imoinda,
the beautiful daughter of a general who had died
in saving Orooncko's life in battle. Their passion, however, was crossed by his grandfather, who,
incensed at the preference Imoinda gave to Oroo-

noko over himself, sold her into slavery. The same fate befell Oroonoko soon afterwards. An English captain, of pleasing address, who came to purchase slaves on the African coast, invited him and a hundred young black men on board his ship. The guests were treated to a sumptuous feast, plied with strong drinks, then lured to the hatches, where they were no sooner confined and chained, than the ship, availing herself of a fair and treacherous wind, sailed away. "Some have commended this act," says Mrs. Behn, "as brave in the captain, but I will spare my sense of it, and leave it to my reader to judge as he pleases. It may be easily guessed in what manner the prince resented this indignity, who may be best resembled to a lion taken in a toil; so he raged, so he struggled for liberty, but all in vain: and they had so wisely managed his fetters, that he could not use a hand in his defence, to quit himself of a life that would by no means endure slavery; nor could he move from the place where he was tied, to any solid part of the ship, against which he might have beat his head, and have finished his disgrace that way. So that being deprived of all other means, he resolved to perish for want of

food; and pleased at last with that thought, and
toiled and tired by rage and indignation, he laid
himself down, and sullenly resolved upon dying,
and refused all things that were brought him."

In this extremity the captain sent a message to
Oroonoko, entreating him to take some food, and
giving him his word that he would set him and
his friends at liberty as soon as they landed. A
promise was sacred with Oroonoko. His own
honour was inviolate, and he had not learned to
doubt that of others—not even of his betrayer.
All that proves more clearly the natural magnanimity of this noble savage is excellently shown by
Mrs. Behn. She never loses an opportunity of
displaying his greatness of mind, his sincerity, his
lofty trust in human virtue. If she erred grievously, if she offended delicacy and morality itself
by pictures not merely coarse but corrupting, it
must never be forgotten that in this sense of the
heroic, of all that is noble and manly, she was
truly great; whether she invented, or merely appreciated Oroonoko, her merit is none the less.

On landing at Surinam, Oroonoko learned of
what value were the promises of white men. He
was sold, as well as his companions, and became

the property of a Cornish gentleman named Trefry,
who called him Cæsar, treated him kindly, and
took him to see a beautiful black girl—a slave
like himself, and in whom Oroonoko recognised
Imoinda, now called Clemene. They were married,
and for a while slavery lost its bitterness. But
Oroonoko was not of a temper to endure his humiliating fate with patience. His power over the
other slaves, who paid him extraordinary respect,
his courage, his talents, and the sullen mood into
which he fell, as he saw the hopes of his promised
liberty delayed from day to day, "gave some
jealousies of him," says Mrs. Behn, "so that I was
obliged by some persons who feared a mutiny to
discourse with Cæsar, and to give him all the
satisfaction I possibly could : they knew he and
Clemene were scarce an hour in a day from my
lodgings ; that they ate with me, and that I obliged
them in all things I was capable. I entertained
him with the lives of the Romans, and great
men, which charmed him to my company ; and
her with teaching her all the pretty works that I
was mistress of, and telling her stories of nuns,
and endeavouring to bring her to the knowledge
of the true God ; but of all discourses, Cæsar liked

that the worst, and would never be reconciled to
our notions of the Trinity, of which he ever made
a jest; it was a riddle, he said, would turn his
brain to conceive, and one could not make him
understand what Faith was. However, these conversations failed not altogether so well to divert
him, that he liked the company of us women much
above the men, for he could not drink, and he is
but an ill companion in that country that cannot.
So that obliging him to love us very well, we had
all the liberty of speech with him, especially myself,
whom he called his great mistress; and indeed my
word would go a great way with him."

Accordingly she tried what gentle argument
and remonstrance would do; but though she got
from him a promise not to make any immediate
attempt at escape, it was given her " with an air
impatient enough to make me know he would not
be long in bondage; and though he suffered only
the name of a slave, and had nothing of the toil
and labour of one, yet that was sufficient to render
him uneasy; and he had been too long idle, who
used to be always in action and in arms. He had
a spirit all rough and fierce, and that could not
be tamed to lazy rest; and though all endeavours

were used to exercise himself in such actions and
sports as this world afforded, as running, wrestling,
pitching the bar, hunting and fishing, chasing and
killing tigers of a monstrous size, which this continent affords in abundance, and wonderful snakes,
such as Alexander is reported to have encountered
at the river of Amazons, and which Cæsar took
great delight to overcome — yet these were not
actions great enough for his large soul, which was
still panting after more renowned actions."

At length, weary of waiting for liberty, he resolved upon flight : he took to the woods, with his
wife and numerous slaves.   Six hundred whites,
headed by one Byam, a man both cruel and base,
followed and overtook them.   After a desperate
encounter, in which Imoinda fought by his side,
Cæsar, forsaken by the other slaves, and trusting
in the promises of his enemies, surrendered.   He
was at once taken and whipped with the greatest
cruelty.   He uttered not a moan, but endured his
fate with a sullen despair that promised revenge.
She whom he called his great mistress found him
bleeding, laden with chains, and suffering intoler-
able anguish, from the Indian pepper which had
been barbarously rubbed into his wounds.   He

said little, but asked for her hands and those of her companions, and, taking them, he "protested never to lift up his to do us any harm." Byam he refused to forgive. "Therefore," said he, "for his own safety, let him speedily despatch me; for if I could despatch myself I would not, till that justice were done to my injured person and the contempt of a soldier; no, I would not kill myself even after a whipping, but will be content to live with that infamy, and be pointed at by every grinning slave, till I have completed my revenge, and then you shall see that Oroonoko scorns to live with the indignity that was put on Cæsar." All we could do could get no more words from him; and we took care to have him put immediately into a healing bath, to rid him of his pepper, and ordered a chirurgeon to anoint him with a healing balm, which he suffered, and in some time he began to be able to walk and eat. But life with him had a purpose, savage though not ignoble. The lash he resolved not to survive, and, if he lived awhile, it was but to be revenged. Before he could attempt this, all he held dear should be placed beyond hazard. His wife and unborn child should not be the prey or the sport of the white man, and only one refuge, inviolate and sure, could he provide for both.

" Being able to walk, and, as he believed, fit for the execution of his great design, he begged Trefry to trust him into the air, believing a walk would do him good, which was granted him; and taking Imoinda with him, as he used to do in his more happy and calmer days, he led her up into a wood, where (after a thousand sighs and long gazing silently on her face, while tears gushed in spite of him from his eyes,) he told her his design : first, of killing her, and then his enemies, and next himself, and the impossibility of escaping, and therefore he told her the necessity of dying. He found the heroic wife faster pleading for death than he was to propose it, when she found his fixed resolution, and, on her knees, besought him not to leave her a prey to his enemies. He grieved to death, yet, pleased at her noble resolution, took her up, and, embracing her with all the passion and languishment of a dying lover, drew his knife to kill this treasure of his soul, this pleasure of his eyes; while tears trickled down his cheeks, hers were smiling with joy she should die by so noble a hand, and be sent into her own country (for that is their notion of the next world) by him she so tenderly loved in this."

But when the deed is done, when his wife is dead, " and past all retrieve, never more to bless him with her eyes and soft language," Oroonoko's thirst for revenge dies in grief. He forgets that he has been whipped, that he is a slave, that Byam, who betrayed him to his ignominy, that the mean wretches who abetted him, still live ; weak, purpose-less, he lies down by the dead and mourns there, every day growing weaker, till he is tracked and discovered. There is great beauty and tenderness in this failure of a great and noble heart, overcome by love and sorrow on the very threshold of its revenge. It is one of those pathetic traits in which the masters of human nature delight; and if it be true, and it bears every appearance of truth, again we must praise Mrs. Behn for having felt its beauty and preserved it. There indeed, in this fine story at least, lay her strength ; she could feel the power and loveliness of truth ; she had the courage, too, to tell it in all its homeliness, and, sometimes, in all its horrible reality. But the ruder and more vigorous times in which she lived could endure the details of coarseness and of bar-

barity which common refinement forbids to ours.
We will give the outlines of Oroonoko's death as
she has told it, we dare not and cannot give all the
particulars of his tragic end. Overtaken though
he was by his enemies, and sinking with faintness,
he was not captured without desperate efforts.

"The English, taking advantage by his weakness, cried out, 'Let us take him alive by all
means.' He heard 'em, and, as if he had revived
from a fainting, or a dream, he cried out, 'No,
gentlemen, you are deceived; you will find no
more Cæsars to be whipt; no more find a faith
in me; feeble as you think me, I have strength
yet left to secure me from a second indignity.'

"They swore all anew, and he only shook his
head and beheld them with scorn. Then they
cried out, 'Who will venture on this single man?
will nobody?' They stood all silent, while Cæsar
replied—

"'Fatal will be the attempt of the first adventurer, let him assure himself' (and, at that word,
held up his knife in a menacing posture): 'look,
ye, ye faithless crew,' said he, ''tis not my life I
seek, nor am I afraid of dying' (and, at that word,
cut a piece of flesh from his own throat and threw

it at 'em) ; ' yet still I would live, if I could, till I
had perfected my revenge ; but, oh, it cannot be !
I feel life gliding from my eyes and heart ; and if
I make not haste, I shall fall a victim to the
shameful whip.' "

Then inflicting on himself a fearful and mortal
wound, which yet left him the power of killing one
of his assailants, he was captured, taken back and
tended till he was well enough to suffer a cruel and
lingering death. When he was fastened to the
stake, he turned to the men that bound him and
said, " My friends, am I to die or to be whipt ?"

They assured him he should not escape with a
whipping. He smiled, and told them since it was
so they need not tie him, " for he would stand
fixed as a rock, and endure death so as to en-
courage them to die ; but if you whip me," said he,
" be sure you tie me fast."

Then asking his pipe to be lighted, he surrendered himself to his tormentors, and died without uttering " a groan or a reproach."

" Thus died this great man, worthy of a better
fate, and a more sublime wit than mine to write
his praise ; yet, I hope, the reputation of my pen
is considerable enough to make his glorious name

to survive to all ages, with that of the brave, the beautiful, and the constant Imoinda."

A popular story, "Oroonoko, or the Royal Slave," long was, both in England and France. Soon after its appearance it was dramatized by Southern; in his dedication of it he expressed his surprise that, having so great a command of the stage, Mrs. Behn "would bury her favourite hero in a novel, when she might have revived him in the scene. She thought either that no actor could represent him, or she could not bear him represented; and I believe the last, when I remember what I have heard from a friend of hers, that she always told his story more feelingly than she writ it."

To that deep feeling of a great wrong inflicted on a noble nature, Mrs. Behn owed the power, the dignity, and the tenderness with which she told the story of Oroonoko; and it is a noble thing and a rare gift to feel the truth with such depth and keenness. Let us compare Oroonoko with the "Grand Cyrus," with the exquisite "Princesse de Clèves" itself, we shall feel nothing there that comes so much home to our feelings, nothing that is so true of every time, as this story. Had Mademoiselle de Scudéry related it, for instance, how differently she would

have told it. Apart from the digressions, the
ingenious episodes, the delicate and graceful
thoughts with which she would have indulged herself, we may be sure that Oroonoko's complexion
would have faded a few shades; he might have
been imprisoned, persecuted, and put to death,
but never whipped; indeed, he would have lived
and died in the attitude of a well-bred man, and
we should have cared very little about him.
Madame de La Fayette's treatment would not have
been very different; if this delicate searcher of
woman's heart could have compelled herself to
treat so wild and tragic a story. It is very true
that in the hands of either lady all the gross and
offensive passages would have vanished; and that,
had it issued from the pen of the latter, Oroonoko
would still be a classic. But though Mrs. Behn's
indelicacy was useless, and worse than useless, the
superfluous addition of a corrupt mind and vitiated
taste—though her style was negligent, incorrect,
and often awkward, and she has no claim to the
rank of a good or a great writer, she had two
gifts in which she far excelled either of the French
ladies—freshness and truth. "Oroonoko" is not a
good book, but it is a vigorous, dramatic, and

true story. True in every sense. The descriptions are bright, luxuriant, and picturesque; the
characters are rudely sketched, but with great
power; the conversations are full of life and spirit.
Its rude and careless strength made it worthy to
be one of the first great works of English fiction.
In some of the nobler attributes of all fiction
it failed, but enough remained to mark the dawn-
ing of that great English school of passion and
nature, of dramatic and pathetic incident, which,
though last arisen and slowly developed, has borrowed least and taught most.

CHAPTER III.

MISS FIELDING.—" DAVID SIMPLE."

THERE is a long gap between Aphra Behn and her successors in English fiction. She was held as a feminine prodigy during the days of the Restoration, and such another even the fertile reign of Queen Anne could not yield. English novels were still doubtful and uncertain productions. They had assumed no definite form—Aphra Behn's tales have none—and though the finely drawn character of Sir Roger de Coverley in the " Spectator " was in itself a revelation, authors and public were very slow to understand it. Swift and De Foe produced wonderful books, but assuredly not novels. " Robinson Crusoe" and " Gulliver's Travels " are unique; but they could found no family, they could not become the parents of a tribe. Sir

Roger de Coverley, on the contrary, is eminently
suggestive. His whims, his gentleness, his unim-
portance as an individual, contrasting with the
minuteness with which he is drawn, the affectionate interest he excites, although there is little or
none of a story connected with him, are all significant marks of the English novel. We may look
in cotemporary French and English literature and
find nothing like him. It took man generations
to paint man as he is. The attempt at anything like fine individual painting is scarcely fifty
years old in France. Up to that time the men
and women of French novels have only a sort of
social conventional truth. The wonderful Gil
Blas himself gives us nothing of the quiet, homely,
and gentle reality of the good old knight. His
reality is that of adventurers, swindlers, actresses,
ministers, and profligate nobles. It is never lov-
able.

It is perplexing that even in England the real
meaning of Sir Roger de Coverley was so long not
understood, or so slow to produce any results.
That so beautiful and promising an opening of the
school that has shown the noble worth of man as
man, was disregarded for years—so far as con-

tinuation goes — seems amazing. We, who are
so much richer than our ancestors, yet value infinitely more than they did the least and faintest
promise of a new vein. Scarcely has novelty appeared in fiction when eager competitors hasten to
plunder and exhaust the rich mine. It does not
seem to have been so in the days when Addison
lived. The delicacy of Sir Roger de Coverley
was not even appreciated, for when English fiction fairly awoke, it was marked by much coarseness and no little rudeness. Richardson is moral,
but he is not delicate or refined, and we must wait
for Goldsmith to find once more the tenderness,
the grace, the quiet though clear power of Addison.

Women were passive enough during this great
change ; we cannot, with truth, ascribe to them an
important part. Yet a part they had, and a very
significant work, if it was not an influential one,
was Sarah Fielding's long forgotten " David Simple."

There are few persons, acquainted with the literary
history of the eighteenth century in England, who
are not also familiar with the name of Sarah Fielding. She was a popular authoress in her own day—
she was the friend of Richardson, and the sister of
England's greatest novelist. Her " David Simple"

was so far esteemed as to be attributed to her brother, who denied the authorship in his preface to
the second edition; and sixty years ago, when it
had been published more than half a century, it
was still a favourite with the public, and the
author's claim to fame.   Who reads it now?—
who even has read it?   Yet it is not without merit;
parts of it can still be read with amusement,
and it is impossible to rise from the perusal of
the whole work without feeling the conviction
that Sarah Fielding was not unworthy the relationship she held to her illustrious brother, and
though not an excellent novelist, was certainly a
woman of remarkable abilities.   Her life, however, has passed, and left as little to record as her
literary productions: a few dates will sum up
what we know of the fifty-four years of her
existence.

Sarah Fielding, born in 1714, died at Bath in
1768. She was the friend of Richardson, and
some of her letters are included in his correspondence, not far from the begging epistle of poor,
starving Lætitia Pilkington; we also find her alluded to by Johnson.

Fielding corrected part of " David Simple," and

Miss Collier assisted her in another work, the "Cry." Her translation of Xenophon's "Memorabilia" is also supposed to have been corrected by Harris. A free, genuine, independent writer, like Miss Burney or Mrs. Smith, Miss Fielding was not. Yet her merit, though it may have been limited by imperfect education, is clear enough to entitle her to some consideration.

In her own circle she was thought highly of, and, spite the adoration in which Richardson lived, he found some literary regard to spare—for of personal liking he was more generous—for the sister of his great opponent. Like all the ladies of his little *coterie*, Miss Fielding worshipped the father of Clarissa.

" You cannot imagine the pleasure Miss Collier and I enjoyed at the receipt of your kind epistles," she writes to him once. " We were at dinner with a *hic, hæc, hoc* man, who said, ' Well, I do wonder Mr. Richardson will be troubled with such *silly women;* ' on which we thought to ourselves (though we did not care to say it), if Mr. Richardson will bear us, and not think us impertinent in pursuing the pleasure of his correspondence, we don't care in how many languages you fancy you

despise us." Then the zeal with which, when he
wants an amanuensis, she presses her services and
claims the honour of making the great Richardson's pen her master. Five or six in the morning
would not have deterred her. What a pleasant
surprise to have found, as she says, "All my
thoughts strengthened, and my words flow into
an easy and nervous style; never did I so much
wish for it as in this daring attempt of mentioning
Clarissa; but when I read of her, I am all sensa-
tion: my heart glows—I am overwhelmed—my
only vent is tears."

Richardson could bear a wonderful amount of
incense; he could return it too, but in a moderate
degree. Miss Fielding was his much-esteemed
Sally, the author of "David Simple." "What
a knowledge of the human heart!" he exclaims,
in this gentle interchange of admiration. "Well
might a critical judge of writing say, as he did to
me, that your late brother's knowledge of it was
not (fine writer as he was) comparable to yours.
His was but as the knowledge of the outside of a
clockwork machine, while yours was that of all
the finer springs and movements of the inside."

The public, however, did not ratify in its full

extent this favourable opinion. Miss Fielding
was thought highly of; she was one of those
ladies who may have sat in the grotto at North
End with Miss Mulso (afterwards Mrs. Chapone),
Miss Prescott, Mulso, and Duncombe; whilst
Richardson read "Sir Charles Grandison," and
Miss Highmore, taking her pencil, sketched the
groups; but her greatest reputation was within the
limits of that *coterie*, and the strongest confirmation
of Richardson's favourable estimate is the denial of
authorship we have already mentioned, and which
Fielding thought himself obliged to give the
public. Three quarters of a century had elapsed
since Aphra Behn had published her "Oroonoko,"
so fresh and vigorous with all its rudeness, when
Miss Fielding produced her "David Simple," in
1744, or, to give the title in full:—

THE

ADVENTURES

OF

DAVID SIMPLE:

CONTAINING

AN ACCOUNT OF HIS TRAVELS

THROUGH THE

CITIES OF LONDON AND

WESTMINSTER

IN THE SEARCH OF

A REAL FRIEND

BY A LADY.

Some of the most remarkable works of fiction
in English and foreign literature had been published during the interval, but not those which
have given the modern novel its peculiar form.
Richardson's career was but in its dawn; Fielding
had only produced his miscellanies and his
" Joseph Andrews" when it appeared; Goldsmith's
" Vicar" did not see the light for years, and Miss
Burney was only sixteen when Sarah Fielding
died. Thus "David Simple" exhibits all the
peculiarities of a yet unformed school, and in that
respect it is a very curious study. There is a
constant struggle going on between narrative and
dialogue, without either being able to find its right
place; we never know exactly what we are
reading,—a sketch of characters or a story. The
title implies that this work, published in 1744,
belongs to the Gil Blas or Picaresca school, and
shows us how that school could be perverted from
its first entertaining and instructive character to
that which suits it least—sentimental morality.
The adventures of a bold, unscrupulous young
fellow, who learns experience by having been the
dupe of knaves, and who is taught how to flatter
by beholding the folly of the wise and the great,

who pushes himself up from the lowest to the
highest ranks of society, and everywhere finds the
same vices and the same weaknesses, because
everywhere he finds men; who has no need to
satirize what he sees, but merely to relate it—for
there are truths more bitter than satire; and who,
as he passes through the various grades of human
life, sketches foibles, absurdities, and characters
with a light but pitiless pen, sparing none, himself
least of all—the adventures of such a man may
not be decorous, but, unless badly told, they are
sure to be irresistibly amusing.

But when a sober and sad young gentleman,
with respectable means, no ambition, and a few
disappointments, travels through a large city in
search of a real friend—when this is his object in
life, and the subject of a narrative, the want of
reality in his purpose, and the monotony of his
pursuit, greatly detract from the entertaining character of the Picaresca school, whilst its funda-
mental defect—the want of a deep personal
interest—remains. No doubt Miss Fielding wished
to write a moral book, but the Picaresca school
does not deal with morality, it deals with truth.
It is not a school in which women can ever hope

to shine, for it requires a good deal more than the intuitive knowledge of human nature which every novelist must possess. It exacts close and accurate knowledge of the world's evil ways, and though these need not be shown, they must be known; purity must be proved in the selection, not in the ignorance, of those sad realities; for it is a trite truth, that to treat parts of a subject well a writer must be master of the whole.

To this deficiency, which she must have felt in herself, we may attribute the somewhat perplexed character of Miss Fielding's novel. It is not Gil Blas throughout, nor is it yet a modern story of passion or domestic life. It is in two volumes, and each volume is unlike the other in construction and incident. We have sketches of character in the first; these are dropped in the second, and we get romantic and melancholy episodes instead. Satirical power is that, however, which lives longest, and strictures on human nature keep a stronger hold on public favour than the most pathetic histories. What made our forefathers laugh keeps the same power over us, but not in an equal degree that which made them weep. Human sorrows are unchangeable, but the gift of delineat-

ing them seems subject to the most subtle and
evanescent laws. It is especially in all that is
pathetic, tender, and delicate that we feel the
changes which feeling and taste have rendered imperative in language; it is in these that we tolerate
least any deviation from our own standard, and
are most offended by those faults of taste which
one age encourages and the next condemns. If,
however, Mr. David's perplexities and misadven-
tures would be found much more entertaining by
a modern reader than the passages in which the
sorrows of Cynthia, Camilla, and Isabella are
narrated, the stories of these ladies certainly display much of that power of character which is the
great merit of the whole book, which caused it to
be attributed to Fielding himself, and which, in his
preface, he praised so highly, though disclaiming all
share in the merit of the performance.

" As so many worthy persons have, I am told,
ascribed the honour of this performance to me,
they will not be surprised at seeing my name to this
preface; nor am I very insincere when I call it an
honour, for if the authors of the age are amongst
the number of those who have conferred it upon
me, I know very few of them to whom I shall re-

turn the compliment of such a suspicion." Then,
alluding briefly to the faults of style into which
want of habit had led Miss Fielding, he proceeds
to say somewhat sharply:

" And as the faults of this work want very little
excuse, so its beauties want as little recommendation, though I will not say but they may
sometimes stand in need of being pointed out to
the generality of readers. For as the merit of this
work consists in a vast penetration into human
nature, a deep and profound discernment of all the
mazes, windings, and labyrinths which perplex
the heart of man to such a degree that he is himself often incapable of seeing through them—and
as this is the greatest, noblest, and rarest of all the
talents which constitute a genius, so a much
larger share of this talent is necessary even to
recognize these discoveries when they are laid
before us than falls to the share of a common
reader."

If, however, as Fielding proceeds to assert, the
characters in "David Simple" were pronounced,
by "one of the greatest men of the age," to have
been "as wonderfully drawn by the writer as they
were by nature herself," Miss Fielding need not

complain of not having been sufficiently appreciated
by her contemporaries, even though a colder posterity did not ratify the verdict. Had this power
of delineating character, which she certainly possessed in no ordinary degree, been concentrated on
one or two principal characters, and made to bear
more directly on the story, instead of being dis-
seminated on insignificant individuals and leading
to unimportant events, the result would, we think,
have been very different.

This particular faculty of giving every individual in a story a definite existence, wholly distinct from his or her importance, is indeed one of
the most remarkable qualities of the modern and
especially the English novel, where the human
being is almost invariably lord of circumstances ;
but it is subject to some stringent laws—the secondary characters must not be better drawn or at
greater length than the more important ones.
This was Miss Fielding's error. She did not seem
to know on what and on whom she should direct her
strength. " David Simple " has all the perplexity
and the confusion of the two schools that evidently divided the mind of the author. The
English school was only beginning, the Picaresca

was in its decline, but both had not yet separated
for ever.   By temperament Miss Fielding belonged
to the English—that school where character is
everything, where incident is only used to develope
character, where the human heart is probed in all
its depths and followed in all its windings.   A
grand school, whether its disciples be the humourists or the more searching investigators of human
motive, but not always an agreeable one, and therefore requiring, in no ordinary degree, the gift of
concentration.   With all their wide differences,
Fielding and Richardson were both its zealous
disciples.

It is not character that rules in the Picaresca
school, it is lively, amusing incident, as shown in
the manners, the follies, the vices of men.   It is
essentially a southern, external school.   It has a
clear vision, but little depth ; sagacity to see, little
or none to divine.   The visible is everything to it,
and to the men and women who move within it.
And according to the teaching of that school, want
of natural discrimination made Sarah Fielding
write.   She had not the gift it requires : character
keenly and lightly drawn, incident ever varied and
ever entertaining, breadth instead of that melan-

choly depth which leaves not a mystery unveiled. Belonging to one school and writing in the other, she could not but fail, if not for the day, at least for the future. And this perhaps shows us more clearly than anything that she came short of genius; that almost unconscious instinct, which leads great minds in the path best calculated to show their greatness, was wanting in her.

Stripped of its complications, the story of "David Simple" is easily told. Two brothers, David and Daniel Simple—one generous and good, the other selfish and base—are briefly introduced to us in their childhood. Their friendship and union suffer no abatement till old Mr. Simple's death, when Daniel, having substituted a forged will for that left by his father in favour of his elder son, becomes master of the property, and treats David with such insolence and harshness that he is compelled to leave the house. Daniel's villainy, however, is soon discovered; David is restored to his rights, and pining for another friend, to replace the treacherous one he has lost, he goes about from lodging to lodging in search of one—sometimes he falls in with a mistress, sometimes he meets with men of wit, in whom he also hopes to find fidelity and tenderness. He is ever baffled, until Valentine and Camilla, a young man and his sister, whom he relieves in the height of their distress, show him that the blessings of friendship and love are not beyond human reach.

Such subjects are apt to be too sweet and to cloy on the palate; against this inconvenience, however, Miss Fielding had a safeguard in a sarcastic turn which frequently reminds one of her brother. As, for instance, the keen and bitter remark which concludes one of the early chapters, when the author informs us that she will leave poor betrayed David to his sufferings, "lest it should be thought," she kindly adds, "I am so ignorant of the world as not to know the proper time of forsaking people."

To David, however, we return with prosperity, and we accompany him in his search for a friend, which, with singular discretion, begins at the Exchange, this being, evidently, the place where friends are most abundant, and most easily discovered. After narrowly escaping being plundered, David is informed that one of the individuals who had attempted to impose upon him is a good man.

" David seemed surprised at that epithet, and asked, how it was, possible a fellow whom he had just catched in such a piece of villainy could be called a good man ? At which words the other, with a sneer at his folly, told him he meant that he was worth a plumb. Perhaps he might not understand that neither (for he began to take him for a fool), but he meant by a plumb, 100,000*l.*"

This sort of satire, however, is better suited to an essay than to a story, and would be more effective in the " Spectator" than in a novel. David's adventure with the jeweller's daughter is of a more practical cast. On leaving the Exchange, he meets with a jeweller, a Mr. Johnson, who asks him home to dine ; he is struck with the beauty and gentleness of his host's younger daughter ; the father perceives the impression she has produced, and, willing to secure a comfortable son-in-law, he invites David to stay some time with him. The young man accepts, and is soon convinced that the friend he is seeking for is to be found in a wife. He pays his addresses, becomes an accepted suitor, and would soon be a happy husband, but for an unlucky contingency. A wealthy old man sees Miss Nancy Johnson, takes a violent fancy to her,

and offers to have her on any terms. Her father
immediately desires her to accept this second suitor,
and discard the first. Miss Nancy rushes up to
her room in a transport of grief, and imparts this
unexpected sorrow to her friend, Miss Betty. This
young lady, who has an eye to the rich old
gentleman, assures her "she should think it no
manner of sin to disobey a father who imposed
such unreasonable commands upon her."

Miss Nancy's reply is frank at least :

" Oh ! my dear, you quite mistake my case; I
am not troubling my head either about the sin or
my father, but the height of my distress lies in not
knowing my own mind; if I could once find that
out, I should be easy enough. I am so divided
by the desire of riches on the one hand, and by
my honour and the man I like on the other, that
there is such a struggle in my mind I am almost
distracted."

Miss Betty upbraids her with an "oh ! fie,
child," and recommends constancy; but Miss
Nancy feelingly tells her, " At what a rate you run
on ! 'Tis easy to talk, but if you was in my place
you can't tell what you would feel !" and she laments
that this good offer did not come first, before she

liked poor David, and when she only received him
because her father bid her, and she thought him a
good match. Her perplexity ends, so far as it can
end, by resolving to let David know her father's
commands, and with the strongest hope that he
shall set her at liberty, and allow her to be a rich
woman, whilst his own heart is breaking. David,
who has unfortunately overheard the dialogue
between Miss Betty and Miss Nancy, goes back
to his own room, where "love, rage, despair, and
contempt alternately took possession of his mind,"
and, raving like a madman, "he repeated all the
satires he could remember on women, all suitable
to his present thoughts, which is no great wonder,
as most probably they were writ by men in circumstances not very different from his."

Tenderness, however, so far prevails over
resentment, that, without reproaching his mer-
cenary mistress, he parts from her on the first
hint, and leaves the house at once. His departure immediately makes Miss Nancy discover
her own mind, and she is distracted for the loss
of her lover. This useless grief soon subsides,
and she becomes the wife of her aged adorer.

This incident is shown with sufficient skill, and

with a certain amount of graphic power, though that is not Miss Fielding's *forte;* but we think much less of it than of the following shrewd and excellent remarks, which, though written more than a century ago, have not yet been sufficiently felt and applied in the world of fiction :—

"I hope to be excused by those gentlemen who are quite sure they have found one woman who is a perfect angel, and that all the rest are perfect devils, for drawing the character of a woman who was neither—for Miss Nancy Johnson was very good-humoured, had a great deal of softness, and had no alloy to these good qualities, but a great share of vanity, with some small spices of envy, which must always accompany it. And I make no matter of doubt, but if she had not met with this temptation she would have made a very affectionate wife to the man who loved her—he would have thought himself extremely happy, with a perfect assurance that nothing could have tempted her to abandon him. And when she had had the experience, what it was to be constantly beloved by a man of Mr. Simple's goodness of heart, she would have exulted in her own happiness, and been the first to have blamed any other woman for giving up the pleasure of having the man she loved for any advantage of fortune, and would have thought it utterly impossible for her ever to have been tempted to such an action, which then might possibly have appeared in the most dishonourable light: for to talk of a temptation at a distance and to feel it present are two such very different things, that everybody can resist the one, and very few people the other."

In this judicious and indulgent discrimination of human weakness lies Miss Fielding's excellence; but we must not ask her to shew it in action—she can analyze shrewdly, but she can scarcely be said to paint well. Inexperience, or want of natural power, continually betray her most praiseworthy efforts, and she would certainly have made a much better essayist than novel-writer.

We doubt if self-deception has ever been more nicely analyzed than in the following speech of Mr. Orgueil to David:

"Whenever I hear a man express an uncommon detestation of any one criminal action, I always suspect he is guilty of it himself. It is what I have often reflected on, and I believe men

think, by exclaiming against any particular vice,
to blind the world, and make them imagine it
impossible they should have a fault against which
all their satire seems to be pointed; or, perhaps,
as most men take a great deal of pains to flatter
themselves, they continually endeavour, by giving
things false names, to impose on their own under-
standings, till at last they prevail so far with their
own good nature, as to think they are entirely
exempt from those very failings they are most
addicted to."

This is excellent, but much better is what
follows:

"But still there remain some suspicions that
other people, who are not capable of *distinguishing
things so nicely,* will think they have those faults
of which their actions give such strong indications.
Therefore they resolve to try if a few words,
which do not cost them much, will clear them in
the opinion of the world."

Mr. Orgueil himself is an instance in point.
David wearies of his company, and takes up with
Mr. Spatter, of whom it is a pity that we have so
little, for he is one of the best-drawn characters
in the book.

He introduces David to the whist-players, whose importance then appears to have been great—takes him at four o'clock to the playhouse, where they have the pleasure of seeing a play damned, chiefly by the author's friends—then introduces him into a critical society, where dramatic matters are discussed by authoritative ladies—and finally takes him to a tavern, where one of the wits talks for three pages, and only stops when his breath fails him. Anxious to make him acquainted with every aspect of society, Mr. Spatter promises to show his friend the Nobodies—that is to say :

" A number of figures of men, whom he knew not how to give any other denomination to—but if he would saunter with him from coffee-house to coffee-house, and into St. James's Park, which are places they much haunt, he would shew him great numbers of them. He need not be afraid of them, for although there was no good in them, yet they were perfectly inoffensive. They would talk for ever, and say nothing—were always in motion, yet could not properly be said ever to act. They have neither wit nor sense of any kind, and yet, as they have no passions, they are seldom guilty of so many indiscretions as other men ; the only thing they can be said to have is pride, and the only way to find that out is by a strut in their gait— something resembling that of the peacock, which shows they are conscious, if they can be said to have any consciousness, of their own dignity."

The two friends go forth, and meet with "whole clusters" of these creatures, and David coming home at night gravely informs his companion that he thinks them quite harmless.

" 'They certainly were created for some wise purpose,' he kindly adds; 'they might perhaps, like cyphers in an account, be of great use in the whole, tho' it was not to be found out by the narrow sight of ignorant mortals.' Spatter made no other answer but by uttering the word 'Fools' with some earnestness; a monosyllable he always chose to pronounce before he went to bed, insomuch that it was thought, by some who knew him, he could not sleep without it."

This habit of constant detraction considerably lowers him in David's mind, and contrasts most unfavourably with Mr. Varnish's unfailing good-nature; this, indeed, Spatter holds very cheap.

"I am confident," he declares, "that he has none of those sensations which arise from good-nature;

for if the best friend he had was in ever so deplorable a situation, I don't say he would do
nothing to relieve him, but he would go on in
his good-humoured way and feel no uneasiness
from anything he suffered. This I say only to
show you how desirous I am of placing things in
the most favourable light; for it is rather my
opinion, he is so despicable a fellow as to lead a life
of continual hypocrisy, and affects all that complaisance only to deceive mankind. And as he is
no fool, he may think deeply enough to know
that the praising of people for what they don't
deserve is the surest way of making them con-
temptible, and leading others into the thinking of
their faults."

This manner of placing things in a favourable
light is not peculiar to Mr. Spatter; it startles
David Simple, but Mr. Spatter settles the matter
by proclaiming himself of a most vindictive temper.

"I think," he declares, "there is nothing so
pleasant as revenge; I would pursue a man who
had injured me to the very brink of life. I
know it would be impossible for me ever to forgive him; and I would have him live only that I
might have the pleasure of seeing him miserable."

David was amazed at this, and said,

"Pray, sir, consider, as you are a Christian, you cannot act in that manner."

Spatter replied, "he was sorry it was against the rules of Christianity, but he could not help his temper."

On this declaration he goes to bed and sleeps soundly, whilst David, thinking him a perfect demon, cannot close his eyes all night, and hastily leaves him the next morning without the ceremony of an adieu. But Mr. Spatter is as great an impostor as the rest. Varnish assures David that his ill-nature dwells in his tongue, and that spite his liberality in dealing out the words "fool" and "knave," he is the best-natured creature living. As to his professions of revenge, they are all false and hollow, this being a passion Mr. Spatter is incapable of feeling.

The same delicate discrimination is shown in the characters of Corinna's six lovers. We have the man of sense who "talked with great judgment on every subject he happened to fall upon; but he had not learned that most useful lesson of reducing his knowledge to practice; and whilst everybody was suspecting him, and guarding against those very deep designs they fancied he was forming, he, who in reality was very credulous, constantly fell into the snares of people who had not half his understanding."

Whilst the name of too much art undoes this gentleman, a fool, thanks to his folly, passes for a " very silly fellow, but one who had no harm in him. Whereas, in reality, he spent his whole time in laying plots which way he might do most mischief . . . . and as his capacity was exactly suited to the comprehension and management of trifles, he often succeeded in his pernicious schemes better than a man of sense could have done . . . I actually knew of several instances of his deceiving and imposing on people in the most egregious manner, only because they could not suspect such a head as his of forming any schemes; but if ever there was a visible proof that he had done any mischief, then the artful man (though perhaps he had never known anything of the matter) had set him on, and it was a thousand pities the poor innocent creature should thus be made a tool of another's villainy, for he certainly could never have thought of it himself."

As nicely contrasted are the man who, by sym-

pathizing with every sorrow and troubling himself
with none, earns the name of good-natured, and
the morose-tempered man, whose heart overflows
with kindness for which he gets no credit. The
impulsive man, who damages every cause by his
vehemence, who is of a very forgiving temper,
"but the worst is he forgives himself with full as
much ease as he does another;" and his opposite,
the hesitating man, who never knows how to
make up his mind until the moment for action
has gone by,—are drawn with the same penetrating
power; but all these delicate sketches lead to nothing, and that power is least shown where it is
most wanted—in the character of the hero.

It is difficult to conceive a more apathetic person
than David Simple in all excepting a moral sensitiveness to right and wrong. After the first
agony he experiences on learning his brother's
treachery, he thinks no more of him; he bears
with the same stoicism Miss Nancy Johnson's
inconstancy. He also falls in love with strange
facility for one of a turn so serious. His second
passion is for Cynthia, a young lady who, after
being hated in her family as a wit, is insulted as a
fool by her patroness. David takes her from this

painful position, and as she has beauty, virtue, and
discretion, he conceives the most reasonable love
for her; but Cynthia's affections being fixed
elsewhere, she hastily parts from him, and he
bears the separation with perfect calmness.

His final love for Camilla is certainly more fervent, but we have no development of passion; it
was not the fashion yet, and more was left then to
the reader's imagination in that respect, than now.
Camilla herself, though we know her chiefly
through her own narrative of her sufferings, is
drawn with great delicacy. The generous girl,
who, free from jealousy, loves her beautiful stepmother for her father's sake—and the cold, perfidious Livia, who ruins her step-children, not from
aversion, but because her interest and theirs are
incompatible,—are painted with the nicest skill, and
yet with that indulgence which we already saw
in Miss Johnson's story. We feel as Camilla,
her victim acknowledges, that Livia's long deceit
on her husband retorts on herself. She has so
long tried to persuade him that his children are
her enemies that she becomes convinced they are
so. Opportunity, too, makes her worse than she
intended to be. She is drawn into actions she

never contemplated, and her husband's goodness
and greatness of mind maked him a readier prey.
It is hard for him to believe her unworthy, since
he loves her, and the man who loves a woman
justifies her intuitively, were it but to prove his
own judgment.

And yet, with all its nice distinctions and
searching analysis, the episode of Camilla's and
Valentine's troubles is not a fortunate one. Livia
stoops to infamy which no writer of fiction would
now venture to introduce in a novel; and in other
parts of the work there are traits of coarseness
which, occurring as they do in a strictly moral
story, and without the least indelicate intention on
the part of the author, remind us significantly of
manners we no longer acknowledge; we must not
heed them, they are but the inexorable marks of
Time—Time which has set its fatal seal on all
that Sarah Fielding wrote.

CHAPTER IV.

MADAME D'ARBLAY.

THE wealthy MacBurneys, of Shropshire, who could probably claim descent from the Irish O'Byrnes, of Wicklow, were the ancestors of Frances Burney. The large landed property of the family was all gone, however, long before she was born. Her grandfather, James, ran away with an actress, was cut off with a shilling, dropped his Irish Mac, and became portrait-painter at Chester; whilst his more favoured brother, Joseph, turned dancing-master, after squandering a noble inheritance. James had a son, Charles Burney, who wrote a history of music, and whose daughter, Frances, will long be remembered as the first English authoress of real celebrity.

She was born at Lynn Regis, of which her

father was then organist, on the 13th of June, 1752, and she died in 1840, having in the course of her long life produced but four novels, though leaving behind her a great name.

Her father, Dr. Burney, was an author and an agreeable man. Frances, his second daughter, was a shy, demure, grave little creature, whom the friends of the family called "the old lady," and who beneath that solemn exterior concealed, not merely an unusual amount of talent, but an exquisite sense of the ridiculous, and a rare and penetrating knowledge of character. Her father relates that "she used, after having seen a play in Mrs. Garrick's box, to take the actors off, and *compose* speeches for their characters, for she could not read them." But this gift was kept for private enjoyment; constitutional shyness would not allow of its being displayed in public, and poor little Frances, who did not know her letters at eight, had another name besides that of "the old lady"— she was called "the little dunce." Her mother, indeed, declared "that she had no fear about Fanny," but this kind, clear-sighted friend died whilst Fanny was still young, and the child grew into girlhood with few advantages of education. Self-educated she appears to have been in the best sense of the word; for whilst her mother read Pope's works and Pitt's Æneid with her eldest daughter Esther, Fanny sat by and listened, and learnt by heart the passages which her sister recited.

In 1760 Dr. Burney returned to London, and took a house in Poland Street. The following year he lost his wife. His son James, afterwards Admiral Burney, was then a midshipman; Charles was sent to the Charterhouse School, and of his four daughters, two, Esther and Susannah, were sent to school in Paris, where they spent two years; Frances was kept at home. She was passionately attached to her grandmother, a Catholic, and Dr. Burney thought it dangerous for her religion to send her to so catholic a country as France. In England she remained educating herself, her father was too busy to mind her much; but listening to his guests did something, for they were amongst the most agreeable and lively wits of the day, and reading freely from his large library did more.

Frances Burney was about fifteen when her sisters returned from France. One of them, Susannah, amused herself in writing a comparative

account of Esther and Frances, that has been preserved.   Esther she describes as a gay, witty, and
lively girl.   Fanny's attributes are "sense, sensibility, and bashfulness, and even a degree of pru-
dery."   What she was then she remained.   Demure and grave beyond her years she always had
been ; the future author of "Evelina," and writer
of the "Diary," appears in that anecdote of the
wig, related by her father.

When Fanny was ten years old, she and her
sisters played with the children of a "hair merchant," their neighbour in Poland Street.   A garden at the back of the house was the playground,
and wigs were the playthings.   One of these,
value ten guineas, fell into a tub of water and was
ruined.   The hair merchant was very angry.

"What signifies talking so much about an accident?" said Fanny.   "The wig is wet, to be sure ;
and the wig was a good wig, to be sure ; but 'tis
of no use to speak of it any more, because *what's
done can't be undone.*"

This juvenile speech is very characteristic of the
cold philosophy Miss Burney afterwards expounded
in her writings.   She began early, for she could
scarcely hold a pen when she first attempted com-

position.   At fifteen she began her Journal.   The
opening lines tell us the purpose of this record:

" To have some account of my thoughts, manners,
acquaintance, and actions, when the hour arrives
at which time is more nimble than memory, is the
reason which induces me to keep a journal—a
journal in which I must confess my *every* thought,
must open my whole heart."

Had the early girlish years of Miss Burney's
diary been published, we might have some insight
into her feelings as a young author; as it is, we
only know that, about the time this journal began
to be kept, Dr. Burney married again, and that
Mrs. Burney soon suspected her young step-daugh-
ter's scribbling propensities.   Fanny was watched,
or, more properly speaking, observed; her retiring
to corners and secluded places was rightly inter-
preted, and clear hints were dropped in her hearing, hints not to be misunderstood, of the impropriety there was in young ladies turning novel
writers.

A sense of duty, may be, too, a fear of detec-
tion, operated on Fanny.   In the presence of her
only confidant, Susannah, who wept at the sacri-
fice, she burned all she had written; even a long

tale, the "History of Caroline Eveleyn," the
mother of Evelina, did not escape. But the card-
table is not more perilous to the gambler than the
pen to the hand that has once indulged itself with
its use. The journal was not enough : it could
not relieve the mind that had told Caroline
Eveleyn's story, and that now perplexed itself
with the fate of Caroline's daughter. What must
become of her, poor thing, between the two social
extremes of her birth—between elegance on one
side, and vulgarity on the other? Miss Burney's
mind was just the mind to enjoy the absurdity of
such a position, even as hers was the talent to
paint it in its true light. Evelina was composed,
and at length written; at length is, indeed, the
proper phrase to use, if we remember that this
story, conceived when Fanny Burney was fifteen,
was published when she was twenty-six.

These eleven years had passed pleasantly
enough for the writer, in her father's house, in
St. Martin's Street—the house where Newton once
had resided. Mrs. Burney was a woman of intellect
and taste ; agreeable friends frequented the domestic circle over which she presided. Arthur Young,
her brother-in-law, Garrick and his wife, Barry,

Mason, Nollekens, Sir Robert and Lady Strange,
and others of less note, were her friends, and her
husband's too. There were also pleasant excursions to Chesington, at Mr. Crisp's—more familiarly
called Daddy Crisp by all the young Burneys—
with whom Fanny was no small favourite. Add
to this, that fine music and fine singing were heard
at Dr. Burney's house, and that he gave his
daughters occupation enough in transcribing his
history of music, for which he took two continen-
tal journeys, and we need not wonder that, between
the happiness, comfort, and tasks of home life,
Evelina slept so long.

But even quiet, demure Fanny got weary of
obscurity. "An odd inclination to see it in print"
awoke within her, with regard to this work. It
was not finished, yet she transcribed it in an upright, feigned hand—she had so often been her
father's amanuensis, that she feared her writing
might be detected, and proposed the incomplete
work to Mr. Dodsley, the well-known publisher,
innocently offering to send him the third volume
" next year." Her sisters were in her confidence,
her younger brother even was in the plot—all
under solemn promises of secrecy; and as in her

letter sent by the post she requested an answer to be directed to a coffee-house, it was Charles Burney who went to seek for it there.

Mr. Dodsley's reply was not encouraging. He declined looking at anything anonymous. Mr. Lowndes, a bookseller in the city, was next applied to. He proved more tractable than the great publisher, and asked to see the manuscript. The first and second volumes were sent to him, and he liked them well, but would not publish them without the third—a most reasonable condition; he even went so far as to say that he would purchase the work.

In time the third volume was completed, but before sending it poor little Fanny had to take an awful step, which conscience and filial duty both commanded. She had to acknowledge to her father the existence " of a little work," and that " odd inclination to see it in print," which Mr. Dodsley's repulse had not daunted.

Dr. Burney is said to have been a pleasant, agreeable man—a careless one he certainly was. He heard his daughter with amazement, laughed so gaily that she could not help joining in the laugh, though against herself, and good-humouredly complied with her request that he would not ask to look at the manuscript.

It does not seem to have occurred to this thoughtless father that by this book his daughter might compromise for ever her reputation or her prospects—for he must have known how futile was her dream of incognito—still less that this shy, quiet little brown lady of twenty-six could possibly have written a tale of merit. He calmly left her to her own prudence and the publisher's generosity. The result of this judicious conduct was that "Evelina" was sent to Mr. Lowndes, accepted by him, and bought for the sum of twenty pounds. The loss of this wise bargain was something like fifteen hundred pounds on Miss Burney's side—so says the diary, confirmed by the extraordinary success of the book. But of that Fanny then thought as little as her father, and the offer "was accepted with alacrity, and boundless surprise at its magnificence."

In January, 1778, Mrs. Burney, who was glancing over the newspaper at the breakfast table, read aloud the advertisement of a new book, "Evelina, or a Young Lady's Entrance into the World." Thus Fanny learned that her book was

out. Her trepidation was great; the work so
jealously hidden from her best friends might
now be in everyone's hands—it might be seen "by
every butcher, and baker, and cobbler, and tinker
throughout the three kingdoms, for the small
tribute of threepence!" as she herself writes in
her diary.

The town soon went wild about the story thus
simply introduced to its attention. Mrs. Thrale
read it, and liked it better than Madame Riccoboni's tales, and that lady then was in the noon of
her fame; she lent it to Dr. Johnson. He was
very unwilling to read it—but once he was per-
suaded to begin the story, he was delighted with
it.

" Why, madam, what a charming book you lent
me," he said to Mrs. Thrale, on finishing the first
volume, and he anxiously asked to know whom
Evelina married. He protested, too, that there were
passages in it that would do honour to Richardson,
and that Henry Fielding never drew such a character as Mr. Smith. True, Dr. Johnson did not
like, or, rather, much admire, Fielding, of whom,
when speaking of this Evelina, he declared that
" Harry Fielding knew nothing but the shell of

life," gallantly leaving Miss Burney the kernel.

The approbation of this great literary monarch nearly sent Miss Burney wild with joy—she confessed to Sir Walter Scott that she could only give vent to her rapture by dancing and skipping round a mulberry tree in the garden.

But, indeed, this delightful " Evelina" fascinated everyone. Burke began it one morning at seven, and sat up all night to finish it. Sir Joshua Reynolds did as much on a day when he had no time to spare, and declared he would give fifty pounds to know the author. Curiosity was strongly excited on the subject : Was it written by Anstey, author of the " Bath Guide " ? Had Horace Walpole anything to do with it ? Was it the production of a man, or was it the delicacy of a woman that had spared it many of the gross passages which disfigured the novels of those days ? The truth was soon known, and Miss Fanny Burney, obscure and unheeded till then, became the prize of fashionable and elegant society.

She went to Streatham, and became Mrs. Thrale's favourite and Dr. Johnson's pet. "Sweet little Burney, dear little Burney," grew to be his familiar and endearing appellations. A charming

place was then Streatham. Mr. Thrale was a
wealthy brewer, an educated man, and a kind
and hospitable one. For many years before he
died his house was the frequent abode of Dr. Johnson, and the resort of many clever, entertaining, and
agreeable individuals; many of that tribe who,
with talent enough to charm in their own day, have
not, however, the gift of bequeathing more than
a half-forgotten name to posterity. Mrs. Thrale
was a delightful woman, lively, full of spirits,
fond of gaiety and pleasure, incapable, indeed, of
any very deep feeling, but frank and fond for the
time being. A pretty woman, too, she was, if we
may trust some of her portraits, with a witty,
careless face.

In this new world, that received her with great
cordiality and equal curiosity, appeared a short,
brown, demure young woman of twenty-six, with
expressive dark eyebrows, and a somewhat large
but most humorous mouth. Spite her reserve
she charmed them all; her diary proves that she
had the power. In this prolix but most agreeable
narrative Miss Burney has painted herself and her
friends to the very life; whether she intended it
or not, she has not concealed two or three of her

own failings—her proneness to satire, her contempt
for intellectual weakness, and her veneration for all
that society esteems; but there is truth in her
keenest portraits, and latent severity in her very
submission to the world's decrees. It is impossible,
after all, not to apprehend her true meaning, not to
acknowledge her integrity, and not to appreciate
the breadth and spirit of some of her sketches,
though they have rather strangely exposed her to
the reproach of flirtation. A woman cannot be
both flirt and prude, in the true sense of either,
and Miss Burney was acknowledged to be prudish.
One fault exonerates her from the other. Besides
being one of the most delightful and lively pictures
of English society in the eighteenth century which
we possess, her diary, so full of charming scenes,
portraits, and sketches of character, is also, and
spite a little though natural complacency, the full
length and sincere likeness of a quiet sensible lady,
with an irresistible fund of humour verging on
satire; not much imagination, and just that happy
amount of tenderness which the owner can always
keep under due control.

Perhaps the greatest fault we can find with
Fanny Burney is that neither her heart nor

her mind seems to have known youth. We
miss its joy and its freshness. She ever was
the same quiet, precise, steady person she lived
and died.

But happy and bright were those Streatham
days when Dr. Johnson called her Evelina, and half
taking her in his large arms, made her sit by him,
and kept her there. He praised her dress, too,
and this was a matter on which the universal man
could be critical and nice to the discomfiture of
untidy ladies. If she attempted to move, he resisted it with a "Don't you go, little Burney;" and
once, on returning to Streatham after a stay in
town, he fondly took her in his arms, and,
as Miss Burney expresses it, "he actually kissed
me!"

Evelina does not seem to have resented it much.
"To be sure I was a little surprised," she writes to
her sister, "having no idea of such facetiousness
from him."

The Streathamites were not single in their admiration of Evelina. When Miss Burney went
home to her father's house in St. Martin's Street,
she received a very characteristic visit from a
known scholar, who has been mistaken for his

better known political namesake, which she has
recorded with characteristic humour.

"In entered a square old gentleman, well
wigged, formal, grave, and important. He seated
himself. My mother (Dr. Burney's second wife)
asked if he had any message for my father?

"'No, none.'

"Then he regarded me with a certain dry kind
of attention for some time, after which, turning
suddenly to my mother, he demanded,

"'Pray, ma'am, is this your daughter?'

"'Yes, sir.'

"'Oh! this is Evelina, is it?'

"'No, sir,' cried I, staring at him, and glad
none of you were in the way to say Yes.

"'No?' repeated he, incredulous; 'is not your
name Evelina, ma'am?'

"'Dear, no, sir,' again quoth I, staring harder.

"'Ma'am,' cried he, drily, 'I beg your pardon.
I had understood your name was Evelina.'

"And soon after he went away. When he put
down his card, who should it prove but Dr.
Franklin."

Mrs. Burney's friends, from Mrs. Thrale down
to Dr. Johnson, induced her to write a comedy.

Murphy approved it, and Sheridan urged it on.
The comedy was written, not without trepidation,
and in its progress it brought the author sugges-
tions and advice, that give us some light on the
stage literature of that day. The great difficulty,
in Mr. Crisp's opinion, was to have wit without
the indelicacy which it seems was then considered
its indispensable accompaniment. "A great deal
of management and dexterity will certainly be
requisite to preserve spirit and salt," writes Mr.
Crisp, "and yet keep up delicacy; but it may be
done, and you can do it, if anybody." Miss
Burney's uneasiness on that head was probably
slight; the comedy was written. "The Witlings"
she called it, but her friends thought it like
Molière's "Femmes Savantes," which she had
never read, and condemned it. It was never
acted.

The subject of this play gives us another of
Miss Burney's characteristics—a strong dislike to
learning in women; not that she thought it objec-
tionable in itself, but the world, which she held in
due respect, laughed at and condemned it, and
she would not differ from the world. Dr. Johnson taught her and Mrs. Thrale Latin, but

Evelina did not delight in her studies. The dread of being thought learned was greater than the pleasure of acquiring a dead language. Many years afterwards she expressed herself even more strongly on the subject. In this, as in many matters, opinion was her conscience. Some interruption to this pleasant Streatham life was made by the sudden death of Mr. Thrale. The brewery was sold, grief subsided after a time, the lively widow resumed her spirits and saw company, and the world went on pretty much as usual with the Streathamites.

In 1782 " Cecilia," which had long been progressing, made its appearance. It proved a more profitable success than twenty-pound Evelina.

Burke called it an extraordinary performance, and the public were delighted with it. " Work hard—stick to it !" wrote kind Daddy Crisp to his Fannikin; "now is the harvest time of your life; your sun shines hot, lose not a moment, then, but make your hay directly." The advice was judicious in both a literary and a pecuniary point of view. Golden successes have their hour, which, once passed, rarely returns. But Miss Burney had kind parents, a pleasant home, and many friends.

She was not in such want of money that she
should give herself up to absolute labour, and
fame she had in plenty. The admiration which
" Cecilia" excited in Mrs. Delany brought about a
curious change in Fanny Burney's life. She was
introduced to this amiable and venerable lady by
Mrs. Chapone, whom she described to her sister
Susan as "the most superiorly unaffected creature,
full of *agrémens* from good sense, talents, and con-
versational powers, in defiance of age, infirmities,
and uncommon ugliness."

With Mrs. Delany herself she was delighted.
They found her alone in her drawing-room at St.
James's Place. " She came to the door to receive
us. She is still tall, though some of her height
may be lost; not much, however, for she is re-
markably upright. She has no remains of beauty
in feature, but in countenance I never but once
saw more, and that was in my sweet maternal
grandmother. Benevolence, softness, piety, and
gentleness are all resident in her face; and the
resemblance with which she struck me to my dear
grandmother, in her first appearance, grew so
much stronger from all that came from her mind,
which seems to contain nothing but purity and

native humility, that I almost longed to embrace her; and I am sure, if I had, the recollection of that saintlike woman would have been so strong that I should never have refrained from crying over her."

Mrs. Delany was as pleased with Miss Burney as Miss Burney was charmed with her; their acquaintance ripened into intimacy and friendship, and finally brought Miss Burney under the notice of Queen Charlotte, who was so well satisfied with the authoress of "Cecilia" as to wish to secure her services as keeper of the robes.

It was a strange fancy. What had literature to do with attiring even a queen? What compensation were 200*l.* a-year, a footman, and Mrs. Schwellenborg's table and carriage, for liberty, time, friends, and intellectual intercourse, relinquished in the very morn of life and fame? The dependence of the lot before her alarmed Miss Burney, but her friends, her father especially, were delighted with the honour thus conferred, unsought for, and with the prospects of favour it offered. Miss Burney consented. Mrs. Delany, who resided in Windsor, was now her dearest friend; the bright Streatham days were over.

Mrs. Thrale had married Piozzi, and as much lost the favour of the world as if by that act she had stooped from the highest station to the lowest. Dr. Johnson was incensed against her for having thus forfeited her dignity, and she broke with Miss Burney for having advised her against this luckless second marriage. Dr. Johnson was dead too, and Miss Burney had entered a new phase, more courtly than literary, which probably influenced her determination. She accepted the office thus offered to her, and, in 1786, began a life of captivity which lasted five years.

It was a hard time. The kindness of the Queen, and the courtesy of the royal family, could not take away their evils from dependence and the ill-temper of compulsory associates, nor yet remove the fatigue of attendance and etiquette. A sad and instructive picture has Miss Burney left of her court life. Her duties were to help to dress the Queen three times a day, to dress herself—no inconsiderable matter in those days of frizzing and powder, when a lady's head, alone, took two hours—and to keep Mrs. Schwellenborg, a vulgar and insolent woman, company. All that is painful and humiliating in

servitude she had to endure; to answer a bell, to
stand behind a chair, to bear fatigue, hunger even
—for attendance often precluded eating, and always
sitting—was the lot before her, and which she had
willingly accepted. She was a servant, and no
royal and gracious kindness could alter the fact.
Literature and liberty both vanished from her life
during those five years. She had no time to
write, and the public ceased to expect her to do
so; of her friends she saw little, of the distinguished foreigners—who knew her from her works,
and would fain have visited her—still less. Royal
dwellings were not to be contaminated so freely
by alien feet. Madame de Genlis came to
England in 1785, and sought Miss Burney's
acquaintance, and Miss Burney then pronounced
her "the sweetest as well as the most accomplished Frenchwoman she had ever met with."

This feeling of admiration for a lovely woman
of most seducing manners, Miss Burney ever re-
tained; but the unfortunate reputation of Madame
de Genlis induced her not to keep up an acquaintance time and circumstances had weakened,
and when she found herself within royal walls,
she carried her prudence so far as not to answer

H 2

" her very elegant little note. Alas! what can
I do?" she added, in self-justification, "I think
of her as of one of the first among women—I see
her full of talents and of charms—I am willing to
believe her good, virtuous, and dignified; yet,
with all this, the cry against her is so violent and
so universal, and my belief in her innocence is so
wholly unsupported by proof in its favour, or any
other argument than internal conviction, from
what I observed of her conduct and manners and
conversation when I saw her in London, that I
know not how to risk a correspondence with her,
till better able to satisfy others as well as I am
satisfied myself."

This was Miss Burney's weak point. She could
defend Warren Hastings without other proof than
the gentleness of his manners to oppose to his
accusers; but then he had the court for him, and
she felt safe. There is, for a woman especially,
great prudence and some propriety in thus abiding
by the world's opinion, but is there generosity?

Madame de la Roche, Wieland's first love and
friend, she was in some sort compelled to see, but
her account of the interview, though most amusing,
is not indulgent, and discarded Madame de Genlis

was still a secret favourite. Her dignity, her
sweetness, the elegance of her manners, and the
delicacy of her praise were regretfully remembered,
in contrast with the somewhat oppressive admiration of the German lady.

Lalande, the astronomer, was not more fortunate
in pleasing this fastidious lady, with whom few
of her professed admirers found favour. " What
a reception awaited me ! how unexpected a one
from a famed and great astronomer ! M. de
Lalande advanced to meet me—I will not be quite
positive it was on tiptoe, but certainly with a
mixture of jerk and strut that could not be quite
flat-footed. He kissed his hand with the air of a
petit-maître, and then broke forth into such an
harangue of *éloges*, so solemn with regard to its
own weight and importance, and so *fade* with
respect to the little personage addressed, that I
could not help thinking it lucky for the planets,
stars, and sun, they were not bound to hear his
comments, though obliged to bear his calculations.

" On my part, sundry profound reverences, with
now and then an ' Oh ! monsieur,' or ' C'est trop
d'honneur,' acquitted me so well, that the first
harangue being finished, on the score of general

and grand reputation, *éloge* the second began, on
the excellency with which *cette célèbre demoiselle*
spoke French.

" This may surprise you, my dear friends, but you
must consider M. de Lalande is a great *discoverer*.

"Well, but had you seen Dr. Shepherd! He looked
lost in sleek delight and wonder, that a person to
whom he had introduced M. de Lalande should
be an object for such fine speeches. This gentleman's figure, meanwhile, corresponds no better
with his discourse than his scientific profession,
for he is an ugly, little, wrinkled old man, with a
fine, showy waistcoat, rich lace ruffles, and the
grimaces of a dentist. I believe he chose to display
that a Frenchman of science could also be a man
of gallantry.

"I was seated between them, but the good doctor
made no greater interruption to the florid profes-
sor than I did myself; he only grinned applause,
with placid but ineffable satisfaction.

"Nothing, therefore, intervening, *éloge the third*
followed, after a pause no longer than might be
n ecessary for due admiration of *éloge* the second.
This had for *sujet* the fair female sex; how the
ladies were now all improved—how they could

write, and read, and spell ; how a man now a days might talk with them and be understood, and how delightful it was to see such pretty creatures turned rational ! "

All this is merciless, but it is exquisite; Miss Burney's genius for satire, and enjoyment of the ridiculous, with her apt penetration of character, appear in every word; but these qualities, which she possessed in so eminent a degree, increase our surprise on learning that soon after this interview, 1788, she began a tragedy, which she finished after leaving that Royal abode in which, with most fervent acknowledgments of great kindness received, she forcibly describes her life to have been " months succeeding months, and years creeping, crawling after years."

Her health was grievously impaired by confinement and the fatigue of attendance ; yet with that selfishness which is habit, not nature, in the great, the queen, though aware of her state, still expected her to remain. Miss Burney, though most careful on this subject, says herself in the diary, " Though I was frequently so ill in her presence that I could hardly stand, I saw she concluded me, while life remained, inevitably hers."

Her resignation, when sent in, was not accepted; the matter was pressed by Dr. Burney, who saw his daughter dying by inches, and Her Majesty yielded coldly and ungraciously. "Traces of internal displeasure appeared sometimes," writes Miss Burney, " arising from an opinion that I ought rather to have struggled on, live or die, than to quit her."

In July, 1791, Miss Burney, whose influence at court had not much benefited her family, returned to the home she should never have forsaken, and left that royal abode where, since Mrs. Delany's death, hers had been a dreary life indeed. A pension of a 100*l.* was the Queen's acknowledgment of Miss Burney's five years services.

Time restored Miss Burney's health; and time, too, brought other changes in her destiny. The terrible days of the French Revolution had come. French princes, dukes, counts, and ladies and gentlemen of noble blood and of every degree, took refuge on English shores, and rarely failed to receive a generous and hospitable welcome. A whole colony of these emigrants settled in Surrey, near Mrs. Phillips, Miss Burney's sister. The tendency to journalize was strong in the whole family, and Mrs. Phillips, who wrote very agreeably, sent full and interesting accounts of her " amiable and charming neighbours," then residing at Juniper Hall.

The Duke of Montmorency, the first of Christian barons ; M. de Narbonne, one of the handsomest and most agreeable men in the old French world, now a fugitive minister ; and M. d'Arblay, his intimate and devoted friend, adjutant-general to Lafayette, were her favourites. M. d'Arblay was a good-looking, soldier-like man, with an open and manly countenance. From immense wealth he was reduced to beggary ; but, as he informed Mrs. Phillips in a first interview, he was not downcast, for Narbonne had something left, and what was Narbonne's was his. A little occasional duelling amongst the emigrants gave variety to this otherwise general communism ; but the pleasantness alone appeared in Surrey at Juniper Hall. M. d'Arblay's frankness, good-humour, and especially his open, soldier-like nature, greatly pleased Mrs. Phillips. Miss Burney, too, was pleased with her sister's account of the little French colony, with which she became personally acquainted at a most melancholy epoch—the death of Louis XVI. on the scaffold. Writing to her father, she mentions M. de Narbonne and M. d'Arblay as having been almost annihilated by the news.

The execution of Louis XVI. proved indeed a European calamity. Republican France cast down that dreadful glove, and made good the cause of her crime by years of heroic contest against every throne. Miss Burney was much affected, and in her letters to her father again alluded to the saddest subject in modern history. "I hear daily more and more affecting accounts of the saint-like end of the martyred Louis. Madame de Staël, the daughter of M. Necker, is now at the head of the colony of French *noblesse* established near Mickleham. She is one of the first women I have ever met with, for abilities and extraordinary intellect. . . . . M. de Narbonne has been quite ill with the grief of this last enormity; and M. d'Arblay is now indisposed. This latter is one of the most delightful characters I have ever met, for openness, probity, intellectual knowledge, and unhackneyed manners."

Madame de Staël appears to have been delighted with Miss Burney. Her warm, generous,

and impulsive temper rendered her advances both
rapid and fervent. Miss Burney's *premier* move-
ment was kind, unless when her penetration into
character rendered her severe; and to mental
weakness she almost invariably was so. She was
struck with Madame de Staël, and attracted
towards one who, though not yet celebrated
throughout Europe as the woman of genius of her
age, was, however, greatly admired. In pretty
notes, written in French English, Madame de
Staël called Miss Burney the first woman in England; and, with less suspicion of flattery, Miss
Burney, writing to her father, thus expressed
herself:

"She is a woman of the first abilities, I think,
I have ever seen: she is more in the style of Mrs.
Thrale than of any other celebrated character,
but she has infinitely more depth, and seems an
even profound politician and metaphysician. She
has suffered us to hear some of her works in MS.,
which are truly wonderful, for powers both of
thinking and expression . . . . She exactly
resembles Mrs. Thrale in the ardour and warmth
of her temper and partialities. I find her impossible to resist, and, therefore, if your answer to

her is such as I conclude it must be, I shall wait
upon her for a week. She is only a short walk
from hence, at Juniper Hall.

"There can be nothing imagined more charming, more fascinating, than this colony . . . .
M. d'Arblay is one of the most singularly interesting characters that can ever have been
formed. He has a sincerity, a frankness, an ingenuous openness of nature, that I had been unjust enough to think could not belong to a
Frenchman. With all this, which is his military
portion, he is passionately fond of literature, a most
delicate critic in his own language, well versed in
both Italian and German, and a very elegant poet.
He has just undertaken to become my French
master for pronunciation, and he gives me long
daily lessons in reading. Pray expect wonderful
improvements."

We do not know if the good doctor expected
what ultimately came to pass, but the intimacy
with Madame de Staël he deprecated. She was
suspected of having been too liberal during the
progress of the French Revolution, and especially
of being still too partial to one of her agreeable
companions, M. de Narbonne. Miss Burney

wished to disbelieve the report, but complied with
her father's advice. Madame de Staël's friendship was declined in such forms as the world
allows; no open breach followed, but some coolness. Both regretted an intimacy which to two
such fine, though different, minds would have been
delightful. In a letter to her dear friend Mrs.
Lock, Miss Burney somewhat naïvely lays bare
that extreme spirit of worldly propriety which
seems to have been part of her being. "I have
regretted excessively the finishing so miserably an
acquaintance begun with so much spirit and
pleasure, and the *dépit* I fear Madame de Staël
must have experienced. I wish the world would
take more care of itself, and less of its neighbours.
I should have been very safe, I trust, without
such flights, and distances, and breaches. But
there seemed an absolute resolution formed to
crush this acquaintance, and compel me to appear
its wilful renouncer."

The world fortunately did not interfere in the
charming French lessons, which ended as most
such lessons end. M. d'Arblay, though poor and
without the least hope of recovering his lost property, made Miss Burney an offer of marriage,

which, on the strength of her pension, and of such prospects as literature afforded, she accepted. Dr. Burney gave a most reluctant consent, and the marriage was celebrated in Mickleham Church, on the 31st of July, 1793.

Miss Burney acknowledged that, in a pecuniary point of view, it was a most indiscreet match on both sides, and confessed that her own surprise at this late and unexpected marriage was "singly greater than that of all her friends united." But experience proved to this staid and precise lady that happiness at least does not go by square rules, since a union which difference of country and religion, and mutual poverty, might well have embittered, was, on the contrary, blessed with more than ordinary peace and happiness. It was attended with sorrows indeed, but they were endurable, for they came from without.

The necessities of her new position quickened Madame d'Arblay's exertions. The tragedy begun under the queen's roof was completed and acted in 1795, shortly after the birth of her only child. It failed, and was withdrawn after the first night. "Camilla," a tale, also begun whilst she was with the queen, was finished in 1796, and published by

subscription. Its success was remarkable: three
months after it had appeared, only five hundred
copies remained of an edition of four thousand.
Notwithstanding the slowness with which she conceived a work, and the length of time which she
took from its conception to its fulfilment, Madame
d'Arblay would now have divided her life between
happy domestic duties and literature, had not
her friends and her husband shaped her life
differently.

She had always had a desire to try her fortune
on the stage, but her friends had advised her not to
produce "The Witlings;" the public had rejected
"Edwy and Elgiva," and now her father, affection-
ately alive to her fame as a writer, interfered and
prevented her from having a comedy entitled
"Love and Fashion," acted at Covent Garden.
With great deference to his wishes, she consented
to withdraw it, and thereby forfeited the 400*l.* she
was to have had for the manuscript. "Cerulia," a
tale which she had turned into a four-act comedy,
had some years previously given him the same uneasiness, and, like "Love and Fashion," been
sacrificed to his fears.

Without intending it, her husband interfered

even more than her father with her literary
career. In 1801, there being peace between the
country of his adoption and that of his birth, M.
d'Arblay went to France. His wife and child
soon followed him, and the war which broke out
in 1803 kept them there all three for ten weary
years.

M. d'Arblay would not serve under Bonaparte;
he was reduced to his *retraite* of 60*l.* a-year and to
his emoluments as *sous-chef* in one of the minis-
terial offices. They resided at Passy, then out of
Paris, and though poor enough, for Madame
d'Arblay's remittances from England were cut off
by the war, they lived in such happiness as the
distracted state of Europe allowed. Madame
d'Arblay made new friends, whom she appears to
have loved tenderly; but her beloved sister, Susan,
had long been dead—she was sometimes years
without hearing from her father, and she wrote
no more those delightful journals which had
formerly been meant for their perusal.

At length, in 1812, under pretence of going
to Newfoundland, of all places, she sailed from
Dunkirk with her son, then seventeen, for whom
she feared the laws of conscription; and the vessel

on board of which she was having been captured by the English in the night without her knowledge —so quietly was it done—she safely reached England. Her transports on finding herself once more in her native land are touchingly told in the journal she then kept. She found her father still living, but very weak and ailing; he had reached his eighty-sixth year. Dr. Burney lived for more than a year after his daughter's return, and had her, if not his favourite child, at least the one most like him in mind and person, by him when he died. Some time before his decease, "The Wanderer," Madame d'Arblay's last work of fiction, begun in France, was completed, and published with hopes of success, which, though not all realized, were not, in a pecuniary point of view at least, all unfulfilled.

The disasters of Napoleon brought the peace of 1814. M. d'Arblay came to England, and took back his wife to France, their son having chosen Cambridge and England as his future portion. The restoration of the Bourbons gave M. d'Arblay some of the rewards of his long and meritorious fidelity to their cause; he was made a general, but did not long survive their second return; he died in England, in 1818, after a lingering illness.

Madame d'Arblay never wrote such touching pages as those in which, a year and a half after her grievous loss, she sadly recorded it. Prepared for the inevitable end, she sat by her husband; he had fallen into a heavy sleep after saying:

"I do not know if these are to be the last words, but this will assuredly be the last thought —our meeting!"

Her son sat with her. She had vague hopes that this sleep portended a favourable crisis; she watched with unwearied patience, and "kept a composure astonishing," she writes herself, "for when no one could give me encouragement I compelled myself to appear not to want it, to deter them from giving me despair.

" Another hour passed of concentrated feelings, of breathless dread . . . . . Alex, my dear Alex, proposed calling in Mr. Tudor, and ran off for him . . . . . I leant over him now with *sal volatile* to his temple, his forehead, the palms of his hands, but I had no courage to feel his pulse, to touch his lips. Mr. Tudor came; he put his hand upon the heart—the noblest of hearts!—and pronounced

that all was over. How I bore this is still marvellous to me ! I had always believed such a sentence would at once have killed me. But his
sight—the sight of his stillness—kept me from distraction!—sacred he appeared, and his stillness I
thought should be mine, and be inviolable!"

Biography should end, like fiction, when the
charm of life is at its fullest, or is utterly broken.
More than twenty weary years did Madame d'Arblay survive this sad breaking of life's dearest tie.
But whom and what did she not survive? One by
one she saw her sisters depart before her, and, saddest of all, she saw her only and beloved son, the
Rev. Alexander d'Arblay, recently appointed minister of Ely Chapel, carried off by influenza in
January, 1837. She survived him three years,
and calmly expired on the 6th of January, 1840, on
the anniversary of the death of that beloved sister
Susannah, "the soul of her soul," as she called
her, and whose loss, forty years before, had made
the seemingly cool and steady Frances Burney
wish herself mad, to escape from the agony of
memory, horror, and grief that then beset her.

Thus ended in comparative obscurity, in days
verging on the present, a life so prolonged, and so

varied in its aspects.   A looker on, and a shrewd
and penetrating one — at fifteen a friend had
well called her "the silent, observant Miss Fanny"
—she acted no important part in the drama of her
times; but what and whom did she not see in her
eighty-seven years?   Dr. Johnson in all his vigour,
which concealed so much goodness and tenderness;
Streatham and the Streathamites, with that lively
Mrs. Thrale, so kind, so reckless, so good-humoured,
so vivacious to the last, who lost the world's favour by marrying an Italian musician, and who
survived this potentate's displeasure, and opened
in person the ball she gave on her eightieth birth-
day.   Decorous Queen Charlotte, and her blooming daughters passed likewise before this quiet,
attentive observer, who, with all her respect, saw
royal as well as plebeian failings.   A few years
later, and she beheld the pale face of another sovereign, not a sovereign then, save in power and ambition, but of one destined to rule, brief though
mighty, and who left on her a never to be forgotten impression, not of soldier-like impetuosity, but
of " care, thought, melancholy, and meditation."
The political vicissitudes, the rank, and the literature of two countries and two centuries mingled

in her long career. Her diary is a list of great
names. From Dr. Johnson at Streatham, from
the opening of Warren Hastings' trial, when she
heard Burke's fervid eloquence poured forth against
her friend, down to Sir Walter Scott's visit, Fanny
Burney and Madame d'Arblay knew, with solitary ex-
ceptions, everyone whom celebrity rendered it worth
knowing. Garrick, Hannah More, Boswell, Mrs.
Carter, Mrs. Chapone, Mrs. Delany, Mrs. Montague, Grattan, Sheridan, Erskine, Wilberforce, La
Fayette, Madame de Genlis, Madame de Staël,
Talleyrand, Châteaubriand, and more than we can
record, sought or met her, and all left their trace
in her quiet life. Rogers the poet brought her
Sir Walter Scott in 1826; and this, one of her
last holds on the literary society in which she had
once been courted, seems to close her active
career. The great novelist's diary thus records the
visit :—

"Nov. 18th, 1826.—I have been introduced to
Madame d'Arblay, the celebrated authoress of
'Evelina' and 'Cecilia'—an elderly lady, with no
remains of personal beauty, but with a simple and
gentle manner, and pleasing expression of countenance, and apparently quick feelings. She told

me she had wished to see two persons—myself of course being one, the other George Canning. This was really a compliment to be pleased with."

Did any other celebrated person after this seek the once celebrated authoress? We are not told so. New schools, new tastes, had arisen in the world of fiction, and the once keen though demure Fanny Burney had entered those still, saddened years of life of which few strangers care to cross the threshold.

CHAPTER V.

EVELINA.

MORE than a hundred and thirty years after the fame of Mademoiselle de Scudéry had reached its acmé, the name of Frances Burney redeemed English literature from the reproach of having produced no woman of genius sufficient to rule, for a time at least, the world of fiction. For some years Miss Burney was certainly the greatest of living English novelists. Her "Evelina" and "Cecilia" had, in their day, as much power and importance as the "Great Cyrus" and the "Princess of Clèves" in another. They were the books which everyone had read, or must read, of which the appearance created delighted surprise or impatient expectation. Goldsmith was dead, and

Walter Scott was not yet in his teens. Miss Burney long stood first. Godwin never had her popularity—Mrs. Inchbald, though more original, and far more pathetic, failed in too many essentials to win an equal position—Mrs. Radcliffe appealed to a lower class of readers—moral teaching spoiled Miss Edgeworth as a novelist. Miss Austin was not popular in her lifetime. We find Sir Walter Scott talking of her to Miss Baillie, not long after her death, as the authoress "of some novels," &c. —neither he nor anyone else could have spoken so of the authoress of "Cecilia" and "Evelina." Her fame was rapid, solid, and widely-spread. It reached Germany and France, and may have extended farther. From the appearance of "Evelina," in 1778, to that of "Waverley," in 1814, no English novel or romance had the good-fortune of equal success.

It is impossible to take up "Evelina" now, and not acquiesce in the correctness of public opinion. We can see in it faults which cotemporaries were more slow to detect—we do not find that it struck out a new path, like Mrs. Inchbald's "Simple Story," or opened a whole imaginative world like Mrs. Radcliffe's romances. "Evelina" is the pure and

womanly continuation of the great school of
English humourists who flourished in the last age.
It has not the strength of Fielding, the sweetness
of Goldsmith, but it has a power of its own—
great reality.

Miss Burney lived in the very heart of the
world of her day. She saw, she heard, and she
painted. Her vision was keen, her hand unerring.
She was too genuine a woman of her times to
appeal to the feelings or to the imagination. No
presentiment of a new school—of still undiscovered
horizons—of regions fair and fruitful—disturbed
her quick sense of the present. Sufficient for her
were the men and women whom she saw, and
their manners, their oddities, their vulgarity, their
coarseness, insolence, or pride. The refinement of
Addison, the pseudo-tenderness of Sterne, the
exquisite delicacy of Goldsmith, were foreign to
her. The spirit of Fielding and Smollett animated
all she wrote. Her delicacy was that of a woman
—it made her works pure, and gave them great
finish—but it was not intellectual delicacy. She
revelled especially in pictures of high-born or
middle-class vulgarity. Her sense of the humorous
and the ludicrous was keen — too keen for

geniality. Her works are cold—hence, we think,
the great falling off in their popularity. Cold,
with all their errors, the great novelists of the last
age were not. They were coarse, offensive, but
their coarseness is like the outpouring of a broad
and genial nature. They write like happy epi-
cures, whose good-humour and mirth efface a
thousand sins.

Miss Burney was not bitter, but she certainly
was not genial. Either her own nature lacked
something in heartiness, or her sense of decorum
checked her, for we find in her no trace of the good
humour which is the redeeming virtue of the
school to which she belongs. Her vulgar people are
not monsters, but there is not a particle of good in
them. Their vulgarity springs from the heart. She
has a keen appreciation of this great social sin, but
it is too severe to be cheerful. Her mannerists are
profoundly selfish. We laugh at them ; we cannot
for a moment endure them. Now, these vulgar
men and women, and fashionable " jargonists," as
she calls them, are the great characters of her tales.
The interest does not rest with them, but the power
does. As she conceived them, they could not have
one good point, but characters more offensive have

been redeemed by one touch of kindness, by some faint diminutive virtue, in the hands of other writers. It is amazing how far a little goodness will go with the reader in some cases. Show us a good man, and the holiness of a saint will hardly content us; but give us a reprobate, with one glimpse of feeling or tenderness, and his place holds good when better men fade away from memory. They who most abhor the devastating career of Alexander are conquered by his magnanimity. He could believe in the fidelity of Philip, and drank, without flinching, the cup said to be poisoned. He had a great soul. He felt trust. One of the most depraved wretches who ever ascended a scaffold after a life of crime was surprised into emotion by inspiring the same feeling. An official, who knew him well, and on whom he called during one of the pauses in his guilty career, was imprudent, and allowed him to see gold—a large sum—in a drawer of his bureau. "Are you not afraid?" significantly asked his visitor. "I am not," was the calm reply. And the man who murdered his friend, who spat on the priest that accompanied him to the scaffold, and left behind him the most cynic boast of iniquity, could not resist this appeal

to his honour : he burst into tears and cried like·a
child.   It was a transient weakness, no doubt of it,
but still it was there—the human feeling that bound
him and made him one in the great brotherhood.
To detect this in the cruel, the ambitious, the hardened, or in the simply mean and selfish, is the
test of genius ; for it cannot be invented, it must be
found.   No one had that marvellous intuition like
Shakespeare ; no one has left such splendid instances of its depth and variety.   But every great
writer of fiction has or should have this gift—it is
Miss Burney's weakness to have failed in it.   Her
heroes and heroines are pleasing and lively, but
they are subordinates ; and her great characters—
the ridiculous, the vulgar, and the selfish—though
very entertaining, do not belong to the depths of
human nature.   They are not superficial, but they
are one-sided. We seek in vain for that something
which reconciles us to humanity in all its forms.
Miss Burney either would or could not—the latter
we believe—take a view so penetrating.   She had
a marvellous insight into certain motives of action
—those that influence the manners, for instance ;
others seem to have been completely hidden from
her view. We must not ask her for the feelings or the

nobler passions. The ignoble she draws sparingly, but with a master-hand.

Her stories are constituted so as to display these peculiarities of her talent. They are made up of strong and entertaining contrasts, often artificially produced, but always amusing. The turn for caricature, which she possessed, is generally a quick sense of incongruities, which escape minds of a graver cast. The very story of " Evelina" is based not on romance, not on love òr adventure, but on the hostile opposition of social rank and manners. Miss Burney's first novel, which she destroyed, was the history of Caroline Eveleyn, a young girl of inferior birth, though refined education, wedded to a profligate young nobleman, by whom she was soon deserted. After burning the manuscript of this story, Miss Burney was struck with the per-plexities to which Caroline's orphan child must be exposed, connected with rank as she was on her father's side, and with plebeian vulgarity through her mother's relatives. And thus, after sacrificing one story, she immediately thought of another, which, fortunately for the readers of her time, and of ours, she began, ended, and did not destroy.

Evelina is seventeen, exquisitely beautiful, amiable, and good-natured, but her prudence is that of seventeen. She has been educated by the Reverend Mr. Villars, who reared her unhappy mother before her. Sir John Belmont, her father, she knows but by name; she is called Miss Anville, and has never seen Madame Duval, her grandmother, and the widow of a Frenchman, or any of her maternal relations, when she visits London for the first time, under the guardianship of Mrs. Mirvan, the mother of her friend Maria.

She is soon seen, known, and claimed by Madame Duval. That lady introduces her to her cousins, the Branghtons, silversmiths, on Snow Hill, and those admirable scenes of triumphant and unconscious vulgarity follow, which every one has at least read once and laughed over.

Vulgarity was indeed Miss Burney's excellence; many other traits she painted with vigour and truth, in this she stood almost alone, and has not been surpassed. Free from the revolting coarseness which then disfigured novels as well as the stage, she followed in all its windings the strange mixture of boldness, insolence, and low taste which is the essence of that unfortunate peculiarity, and makes something of it very like a vice.

Many authors, in attempting vulgarity, have
simply painted a want of refinement — Miss
Burney has struck home; and if we did not know
it before, we know it in reading her pages—vulgarity is selfish and mean.

Ever since the age of fifteen, Miss Burney had
been in the habit of keeping a diary. She had
learned the difficult art of relating clearly and
amusingly whatever passed around her. The
facility she had acquired strengthened the wish of
writing an epistolary novel. All the perplexities
of Evelina are known to us by her letters.
We thus have, in all their keenness and misery, the
numberless troubles which beset susceptible youth
on its first contact with coarseness and insolence.
The vivacity of her sensations gives new force to
all that Evelina tells us. The Branghtons
appear to us as they appear to her, a refined,
delicate girl, whom experience has not made
lenient. The picture, which is severe in "Cecilia"
when the author speaks, is far less so when
Evelina only relates her strong but very justi-
fiable impressions of those unfortunate relatives.
She is prejudiced no doubt, but we can at least
share her prejudices, for she is aggrieved. We

have less sympathy with Miss Burney's. The relatives to whom Evelina is introduced by her grandmother, Madame Duval, are not such as to fascinate a fastidious girl of seventeen, and her account of them is not partial.

"Mr. Branghton appears about forty years of age. He does not seem to want a common understanding, though he is very contracted and prejudiced; he has spent his whole time in the City, and I believe feels a great contempt for all who reside elsewhere.

" His son seems weaker in his understanding, and more gay in his temper; but his gaiety is that of a foolish, overgrown schoolboy, whose mirth consists in noise and disturbance. He disdains his father for his close attention to business and love of money; though he seems himself to have no talents, spirit, or generosity to make him superior to either. His chief delight appears to be tormenting and ridiculing his sisters; who, in return, most heartily despise him.

"Miss Branghton, the eldest daughter, is by no means ugly: but looks proud, ill-tempered, and conceited. She hates the City, though without knowing why; for it is easy to discover she has lived nowhere else.

"Miss Polly Branghton is rather pretty, very ignorant, very giddy, and, I believe, very good-natured."

The good-nature of Miss Polly vanishes on nearer view, and all the offensive peculiarities of the family increase.

Madame Duval relates her grand-daughter's story to this tribe of cousins, and their comments, though not ill-meant, are offensive.

"In a few minutes, Miss Branghton, coming suddenly up to her sister, exclaimed, 'Lord, Polly, only think! Miss never saw her papa!'

"'Lord, how odd!' cried the other; 'why, then, Miss, I suppose you wouldn't know him?'"

This is vulgarity in all its coarseness. The foolish wonder—the ill-bred and unfeeling question—would make us know the Miss Branghtons, had they not already been described for us. Miss Burney excelled in these home-thrusts. She had the rapid and decisive touch of genius. Now that the secrets of her manner are known, and have been exhausted, we may think too little of her application of the method. Any tyro in novel writing could do as much and almost as well;

but hers is still the irresistible charm of priority, its freshness and its vigour. No vulgar girls can surpass her Miss Branghtons. Their exclamations, when they learn that their cousin has danced with Lord Orville, are the very quintessence of the low, vulgar admiration of rank and station.

"'Lord, Polly! only think—Miss has danced with a lord!'

"'Well,' cried Polly, 'that's a thing I should never have thought of!—and pray, Miss, what did he say to you?'"

The distinction between the envious elder sister and the foolish younger one is kept up, even in this short and exquisitely characteristic passage. We need not wonder that "Miss," as they call Evelina, is not enchanted with such cousins, and that, on being asked to call upon them at Snow-hill, she exclaims mentally—"I wish we may not meet again till that time arrives."

But meet they must, and often. They go to the Opera together; and Mr. Branghton, on putting down a guinea and learning that it will only pay for two places, takes it up, and kindly informs the doorkeeper "it will be long enough before he'll see it again." He takes them all to the gallery,

and is equally amazed and indignant at what he
gets for his money.

"'I was never so fooled out of my money
before, since the hour of my birth. Either the
doorkeeper's a knave, or this is the greatest im-
position that ever was put upon the public.'

"'*Ma foi!*' cried Madame Duval, 'I never sat
in such a mean place in all my life. Why, it's as
high—we shan't see nothing.'

"'I thought at the time,' said Mr. Branghton,
'that three shillings was an exorbitant price for a
place in the gallery; but as we'd been asked so
much at the other doors, why, I paid it without
many words; but then, to be sure, thinks I, it
can never be like any other gallery; we shall see
some *crincum crankum* or other for our money;
but I find it's as arrant a take-in as ever I met
with.'

"'Why, it's as like the twelve-penny gallery at
Drury Lane,' cried the son, 'as two peas are to
one another. I never knew father so bit before.'

"'Lord,' said Miss Branghton, 'I thought it
would have been quite a fine place—all over, I
don't know what—and done quite in taste.'"

The nature of the entertainment heightens the

indignation of the family.   They agree in deriding
it, and this similarity of opinion is almost like
family union.   Constant jarring is one of the
forms their vulgarity most affects.

Evelina surprises them taking tea in the rooms
on the second floor of their house—the first is let
—and their annoyance is expressed by rude re-
crimination.

"'Goodness,' cried young Branghton, 'if there
isn't Miss!'

"'Lord! so there is,' said Miss Polly; 'well,
I'm sure, I should never have dreamed of Miss's
coming.'

"'Nor I neither, I'm sure,' cried Miss Branghton; 'or else I would not have been in this room
to see her.   I'm quite ashamed about it—only not
thinking of seeing anybody but my aunt—however,
Tom, it's all your fault; for you knew very well
I wanted to borrow Mr. Smith's room, only you
were so *grumpy*, you would not let me.'"

The two sisters can also be *grumpy*, even without provocation.   Miss Branghton informs Evelina
privately that a young man whom she has just
seen is named Brown, is a haberdasher, and is
Polly's lover.   She is disgusted herself with the

meanness of the match, but Polly has no spirit.

" ' And for that matter,' added she, ' I believe Polly herself don't care much for him, only she's in such a hurry to be married before me; however, she's very welcome, for I'm sure I don't care a pin's point whether I ever marry at all—it's all one to me.'

" Some time after this, Miss Polly contrived to tell *her* story. She assured me, with much tittering, that her sister was in a great fright lest she should be married first. ' So I make her believe that I will,' continued she, ' for I love dearly to plague her a little; though, I declare, I don't intend to have Mr. Brown in reality; I'm sure I don't like him half well enough—do you, Miss ?'

" ' It is not possible for me to judge of his merits,' said I, 'as I am entirely a stranger to him.

" ' But what do you think of him, Miss ?'

" ' Why, really I—I don't know.'

" ' But do you think him handsome ?—some people reckon him to have a good, pretty person; but I'm sure, for my part, I think he's monstrous ugly—don't *you*, Miss ?'

" ' I am no judge; but I think his person is very—very well.'

" ' *Very well !* Why, pray, Miss,' in a tone of vexation, ' what fault can you find with it ?'

" ' Oh ! none at all.'

" ' I'm sure you must be very ill-natured if you could. Now there's Biddy says she thinks nothing of him—but I know it's all out of spite. You must know, Miss, it makes her as mad as can be, that I should have a lover before her; but she's so proud that nobody will court her, and I often tell her she'll die an old maid. But the thing is, she has taken it into her head to have a liking for Mr. Smith as lodges on the first floor; but, Lord, he'll never have her, for he's quite a fine gentleman, and besides, Mr. Brown heard him say one day that he'd never marry as long as he lived, for he'd no opinion of matrimony.'

" ' And did you tell your sister this ?'

" ' To be sure, I told her directly; but she did not mind me; however, if she will be a fool, she must.' "

Evelina has the happiness of meeting this obstinate bachelor. He was asked to lend his room for dinner, but though Miss Branghton preferred the request, he prudently refused. " However," adds Miss Polly, " we shall have it to drink tea in, and then, perhaps, you may see him; and I assure you he's quite like one of the quality, and dresses as fine, and goes to balls and dances, and everything quite in taste; and besides, Miss, he keeps a footboy of his own, too."

Whilst waiting for Mr. Smith's room, Miss Polly suggests that they shall go down *to shop*, and see the people go by.

" ' Lord, Polly,' said the brother, ' you're always wanting to be staring and gaping; and I'm sure you needn't be so fond of showing yourself, for you're ugly enough to frighten a horse.'

" ' Ugly, indeed! I wonder which is best, you or me? But I tell you what, Tom, you've no need to give yourself such airs; for if you do, I'll tell Miss of—you know what'——

" ' Who cares if you do? You may tell what you will, I don't mind'——

" ' Indeed,' cried I, ' I do not desire to hear any secrets.'

" ' Oh! but I am resolved I'll tell you, because Tom's so very spiteful. You must know, t'other night'——

" ' Polly!' cried the brother, ' if you tell of that, Miss shall know all about your meeting young

Brown—you know when—so I'll be quits with
you, one way or other.'

" Miss Polly coloured, and again proposed our
going downstairs till Mr. Smith's room was ready
for our reception.

" ' Ay! so we will,' said Miss Branghton ; ' I'll
assure you, cousin, we have some very genteel
people pass by our shop sometimes. Polly and I
always go and sit there when we've cleaned ourselves.'

" ' Yes, Miss,' cried the brother, ' they do
nothing all day long, when father don't scold them.
But the best fun is, when they've got all their
dirty things on, and all their hair about their ears ;
sometimes I send young Brown upstairs to them,
and then there's such a fuss ! There they hide
themselves, and run away, and squeel and squall
like anything mad ; and so then I puts the two
cats into the room, and I gives them a good whipping, and so that sets them a-squalling too ; so
there's such a noise and such an uproar—Lord,
you can't think, Miss, what fun it is !'

" This occasioned a fresh quarrel with the sisters ; at the end of which it was at length decided
that we should go to the shop.

"In our way downstairs, Miss Branghton said aloud—

"'I wonder when Mr. Smith's room will be ready?'

"'So do I,' answered Polly; 'I'm sure we should not do any harm to it now.'"

The hint is thrown away; Mr. Smith will not open his room till tea-time. That gentleman's good breeding is on a par with that of Tom or Polly. His apology to Evelina for not giving the room sooner is frank—

"Why, ma'am, the truth is, Miss Biddy and Polly take no care of anything; else, I'm sure, they should be always welcome to my room, for I'm never so happy as in obliging the ladies— that's my character, ma'am; but really, the last time they had it, everything was made so greasy and so nasty that, upon my word, to a man who wishes to have things a little genteel, it was quite cruel."

This devoted squire of dames is smitten with Evelina, and testifies his admiration in terms as polite as those of his apology.

"One place is the same as another to me, so that it be but agreeable to the ladies. I would go anywhere with you, ma'am (to me), unless, indeed,

it were to *church* ; —ha, ha, ha !—you'll excuse me,
ma'am ; but, really, I never could conquer my fear
of a parson—ha, ha, ha ! Really, ladies, I beg
your pardon for being so rude; but I can't help
laughing, for my life."

This agreeable theme Mr. Smith takes care to
renew on other occasions. He kindly assures
Evelina that he has no bad intentions, but
that she must be patient. "Really, there is no
resolving upon matrimony all at once : what with
the loss of one's liberty, and what with the ridicule of all one's acquaintance,—I assure you,
ma'am, you are the first lady who ever made me
even demur upon this subject; for, after all, my
dear ma'am, marriage is the devil."

Evelina's short and sharp reply does not en-
lighten Mr. Smith. "To be sure," he kindly
observes, "marriage is all in all with the ladies ;
but with us gentlemen it's quite another thing.
Now, only put yourself in my place ; suppose you
had such a large acquaintance of gentlemen as I
have, and that you had always been used to appear
a little—a little smart among them—why, now,
how should you like to let yourself down all at
once into a married man ?"

The folly, the confident impudence of Mr. Smith, his "vulgarness," as Madame Duval would say, seemed to Dr. Johnson the very height of art. He would not admit that Fielding could have drawn such a character. It is hard to grant as much, for Johnson was prejudiced, and we need not be so; but one thing is certain, Fielding *would* not have drawn Mr. Smith—no man would. Mr. Smith, like Miss Burney's Sir Robert Floyer—like Miss Edgeworth's Sir Philip Baddeley—like Miss Austin's Rev. Mr. Collins—is woman's revenge of many a slight and many an insult, keenly felt, but never openly resented. These gentlemen display to our ridicule and scorn the long triumphant insolence with which coarse and ill-bred men choose to treat women. Without any effort, any interference on the part of the author, they wilfully rush on to their fate. The presumption of Mr. Smith, his fear of a parson, his polite "for, after all, my dear ma'am, marriage is the devil;" his kind sympathy with the matrimonial propensities of the female sex, "To be sure, marriage is all in all with the ladies;" then that feeling appeal to Evelina's sense of right, that request to the lovely, high-bred, accomplished girl to put herself in the place

of a low, vulgar, foolish city *beau,* and sympathize
with the downfall in his position and consequence
marriage must produce, are instances of absurdity
and unconscious insolence which condemn him to
pitiless ridicule. It is almost supererogatory to show
us how the mere approach of Evelina's aristocratic
friends abashes and sinks him down into conscious
inferiority.

The superiority which Miss Burney showed in
her wonderful delineations of vulgar men and women did not reach fashionable society. Yet, if we
compare her representation with that of the modern
fashionable novel, with its foolish descriptions of
foolish people and foolish balls, we are struck with her
spirit and her vigour. The slightest incidents of
society as painted by her have a charm which cannot lie in themselves. Men and women who live
for little more than pleasure are invested with a
graceful individuality. For such characters as Sir
Clement Willoughby, insolent and polished, Miss
Burney had an evident weakness. She forgave
much to the charm of manner. They occur not
merely in her works, but are to be found in her
diary, sketched to the very life, free, capricious,
and delightful, spite of all their delinquencies and

failures.   Sir Clement's, indeed, are carried to an
extreme.   His passion for Evelina is alternately
bold and perfidious, and always impertinent, yet,
with it all, the impression left is that of such good
breeding as lies in manner, superficial indeed, but
captivating.   It was a more difficult task to paint
the hero, Lord Orville, for he was to be perfect.
Yet he is no more insipid than the vivacious
Evelina herself.   He is the handsome, gallant, polite, and ardent lover every such girl as Evelina
hopes to find on entering life.   He is rich, titled,
and universally admired ; no drawback with Evelina, who is neither very unworldly nor very independent.   Her admiration of him is shown, in a
very innocent though dangerous manner, at her
first London ball.   A fop, one of the mannerists
Miss Burney delighted to display, asks her to
dance.   She declines, and almost immediately
afterwards accepts Lord Orville's hand.   He is
twenty-six, " gaily but not foppishly dressed, and,
indeed, extremely handsome, with an air of mixed
politeness and gallantry."   Who could resist him?
The impropriety of her conduct brings Evelina
into some trouble; she has also the mortification
of knowing that her bashfulness has caused his

lordship to form no very favourable opinon of her
understanding. "A poor, weak girl," is his verdict.
Yet their acquaintance progresses. They meet at
public places, and he delicately protects her against
her injured dancer's insolence, or Sir Clement
Willoughby's too ardent admiration. In vain the
Reverend Mr. Villars sees the danger from his
Dorsetshire parsonage. Evelina cannot be warned.
She is under a spell which supposed unworthiness
and absence for a while suspend, but which Lord
Orville's presence quickly renews. They meet,
no longer with the Branghtons of Snowhill, with
a coarse Captain Mirvan or a Madame Duval, to
interfere, but at a watering-place surrounded with
fashionable society. They are inmates of the same
house, and nothing can exceed Evelina's happiness.
The openness with which she reveals it to her kind
guardian has something very fresh and charming.
She seems unconscious of her own secret, and his
gentle remonstrances first reveal to her the progress of a passion she never suspected. "Young,
animated, entirely off your guard, and thoughtless
of some consequences, *imagination* took the reins;
and *reason*, slow-paced, though sure-footed, was
unequal to the race of so eccentric and flighty a
companion. How rapid was then my Evelina's

progress through those regions of fancy and passion whither her new guide conducted her! She
saw Lord Orville at a ball, and he was *the most
amiable of men!* She met him again at another,
and *he had every virtue under heaven !*"

The Reverend Mr. Villars is right enough—
Evelina's is not the lofty love built on well-grounded
esteem, but it is young, happy love, and we are
pleased that it should be crowned with every bless-
ing. Scarcely has she perceived her danger, and
resolved to treat Lord Orville with coldness, when
a declaration of his affection removes the necessity
for this restraint. Almost in one moment she recovers her father, Sir John Belmont, who had
been deceived into acknowledging her foster-
sister for his daughter, and she becomes Lady
Orville.

The tale ends like a fairy tale ; the splendours
of this world are added to its choicest blessings.
We have learned to think this too sweet, but it is
the genuine conclusion of the novel of those days :
love in a cottage was its theory, no doubt, but love
with a coronet, and a coach and four, was its invari-
able practice.

Apart from its merit, Evelina is valuable
and interesting as a woman's picture of Eng-

lish life and society in the year 1778. It is
much more minute than any man's novel of that
age; and that minuteness, one of the modern characteristics of fiction, if it did not come in with
women, is assuredly the offspring of domestic life.
The close attention she bestowed on everything
enabled Miss Burney to give us a curious and
faithful picture of life as she saw it. The form
which the vulgarity of the Branghtons affects has
passed away, unchangeable though the spirit must
ever be. Even the matchless "Lord, Polly! only
think, Miss has danced with a lord!" leads us into
the remote past, or sinks us several grades lower
in society. The amusements she describes through
Evelina also speak of another age and of bygone
manners. We can realize the wonderful presence
of Garrick, and imagine the opera; but the strange
assemblies, gardens, and exhibitions, whose very
names sound unfamiliar, warn us that more than
three quarters of a century have passed over Evelina and her friends. Our pleasure in reading partakes of an antiquarian's; these are the vicissitudes
of present pictures; they fade away ere the ink
with which they are written is well nigh dry.

But to paint these, and passing manners, follies,

and vanities, is the irresistible bent of some minds.
Miss Burney had little or no imagination. Her
novels, whether in town or country, whether the
matter be ridiculous or painful, show no glimpse
of nature, and scarcely betray a touch of tenderness. Manners, the manners she saw, were her
forte, and this excellence, though secondary, renders
her the best exponent of the town life and society of
her age. No one has left us pictures so complete,
no one has drawn so distinctly classes of fashionable society, of which all record has vanished save
such as is to be found in her pages. Richardson's
society is acknowledged to be formal and fictitious;
Smollett and Fielding are too coarse, and sink to
regions and adventures too degrading; Goldsmith
painted human nature; Sterne invented a world
of his own; we can learn much from them, but
from none so much of the external social aspect
of a certain narrow but definite portion of the
eighteenth century as from Miss Burney.

CHAPTER VI.

CECILIA.

To possess a power is almost always to be conscious of it. No one knew better than Miss Burney what she could do, or how to select subjects that displayed her excellence.

Her second novel, " Cecilia," though it has not the charm and the seduction of " Evelina," is, even more than that pleasing tale, an acute mirror of the passing follies of the day. It is admirably adapted to display Miss Burney's faculty for bringing out forcibly the weaknesses and ridicules of men and women, and so long as the incidents are chosen with reference to those two objects, the tale remains excellent.

Cecilia is a beautiful and accomplished heiress

of twenty. A few months more will put her in
possession of an estate with a rental of three thousand a year, and clogged by only one condition,
th'at the happy possessor of her hand shall also
assume her surname of Beverley. From this, and
from the accident of being left for a few months
to the guardianship of three gentlemen of very
different tempers, spring all the troubles of the
beautiful orphan. The three guardians are admirably drawn. Mr. Briggs is a sordid miser,
Mr. Harrel is extravagant to profligacy, and Mr.
Delvile, a gentleman of ancient birth and pompous pride, can never recover the surprise into
which he is thrown at finding himself in conjunction with two such individuals. That the Dean,
Cecilia's uncle, should have been " so little conver-
sant with the distinctions of the world as to disgrace him with inferior coadjutors," is to him a
source of ever new amazement, with which he entertains Cecilia whenever they meet. Whatever
may be the subject of discourse between them,
this extraordinary mistake of the Dean's is introduced as a matter of wonder and comment. How
could the Dean ever come to think of it? That
anyone should have dreamt of associating Mr.

Delvile with a Mr. Harrel, the grandson of a
steward, with a Mr. Briggs, a low-born, grovelling
miser, is one of those subjects for meditation
which minds like Mr. Delvile's cannot easily
exhaust.

His contempt is heartily returned by Mr.
Briggs, who irreverently calls him Don Puffabout,
and who, being "a warm man," esteems and loves
himself all the more for this wealth. Mr. Harrel
does not trouble himself about either of his coadjutors. Cecilia, his wife's early friend, lives under
his roof; she is his prize, and no one can deny that
he makes the best of his opportunities. Mr.
Harrel's house in Portman Square is one of the
gayest in town. Cecilia is introduced to routs
and masquerades; fortune-hunters and lovers,
attracted by her wealth and beauty, importune her
with their admiration, and we are brought into
some very amusing scenes and some foolish company, showing us that fashionable society in 1782
was not very unlike what it is in our own
days.

The foolish volubility of Miss Larolles, the
supercilious stupidity of Miss Leeson, are admirably drawn; and Captain Aresby and Mr.

Meadows, though merely sketches of mannerists, are none the less excellent.

"Among the gentlemen, the most conspicuous, by means of his dress, was Mr. Aresby, a captain in the militia; a young man who, having frequently heard the words 'red-coat' and 'gallantry' put together, imagined the conjunction not merely customary but honourable, and therefore, without even pretending to think of the service of his country, he considered a cockade as a badge of politeness, and wore it but to mark his devotion to the ladies, whom he held himself equipped to conquer and bound to adore."

Captain Aresby is also a "jargonist." His language consists of set phrases intermixed with set French words. "The *tout ensemble*," as he himself would say, "is most petrifying." The man-hater, a Mr. Albany, who goes about telling disagreeable truths, is Captain Aresby's particular aversion, and gives him an excellent opportunity of displaying the graces of his dialect. "He is a most petrifying wretch, I assure you. I am *obsedé* by him *partout;* if I had known he had been so near, I should certainly have said nothing."

" 'Where is it, then,' said Cecilia, 'that you have so often met him ?'

" ' Oh !' answered the captain, ' *partout*, there is no greater bore about town. But the time I found him most petrifying was once when I happened to have the honour of dancing with a very young lady, who was but just come from a boarding-school, and whose friends had done me the honour to fix upon me, upon the principle of first bringing her out; and while I was doing *mon possible* for killing the time, he came up, and, in his particular manner, told her I had no meaning in anything I said. I must own I never felt more tempted to be *enragé* with a person in years in my life.' "

Mr. Meadows is quite another sort of man. He is an *ennuyé*, and in him we see the dawn of Glenthorn and the satire of the Byronian hero of later times, minus the passion.

" The first person that addressed them was Captain Aresby, who, with his usual delicate languishment, smiled upon Cecilia, and softly whispering, ' How divinely you look to-night!' proceeded to pay his compliments to some other ladies.

" ' Do, pray now,' cried Miss Larolles, ' observe

Mr. Meadows; only just see where he has fixed himself—in the very best place in the room, and keeping the fire from everybody! I do assure you that's always his way, and it's monstrous provoking, for if one's ever so cold he lollops so that one's quite starved. But you must know there's another thing he does that is quite as bad, for if he gets a seat he never offers to move, if he sees one sinking with fatigue. And besides, if one is waiting for one's carriage two hours together, he makes it a rule never to stir a step to see for it. Only think, how monstrous!'

" 'These are heavy complaints indeed,' said Cecilia, looking at him attentively; 'I should have expected from his appearance a very different account of his gallantry, for he seems dressed with more studied elegance than anybody here.'

" ' Oh, yes!' cried Miss Larolles; 'he is the sweetest dresser in the world; he has the most delightful taste you can conceive, nobody has half so good a fancy. I assure you it's a great thing to be spoke to by him; we are all of us quite angry when he won't take any notice of us.'

" ' Is your anger,' said Cecilia, laughing, ' in honour of himself or of his coat ? '

" 'Why, Lord, don't you know all this time that he is an *ennuyé*?'

" 'I know at least,' answered Cecilia, 'that he would soon make one of me.'

" 'Oh, but one is never affronted with an *ennuyé*, if he is ever so provoking, because one always knows what it means.'

" 'Is he agreeable?'

" 'Why, to tell you the truth—but pray, now, don't mention it—I think him most excessive disagreeable. He yawns in one's face every time one looks at him. I assure you, sometimes I expect to see him fall fast asleep while I am talking to him —for he is so immensely absent he don't hear one half that one says; only conceive how horrid!'"

Mr. Meadows's dancing is even worse than his conversation, according to Miss Larolles. Of all things she advises Cecilia never to dance with this absent partner, whom even a minuet cannot render attentive.

The Heiress and the Ennuyé meet in the course of the story; but, after an absent conversation, Mr. Meadows, forgetting that he is addressing a lady, gets up and walks away. A friend accosts him :—

" ' Why, Meadows, how's this?—are you caught at last ?'

" ' Oh, worn to death!—worn to a thread!' cried he, stretching himself, and yawning. ' I have been talking with a young lady to entertain her! Oh, such heavy work! I would not go through it again for millions !'

" ' What! have you talked yourself out of breath ?'

" ' No, but the effort!—the effort! Oh, it has unhinged me for a fortnight! Entertaining a young lady!—one had better be a galley-slave at once !'

" ' Well, but did she not pay your toils?—she is surely a sweet creature.'

" ' Nothing can pay one for such insufferable exertion. Though she's well enough, too—better than the common run--but shy, quite too shy; no drawing her out.'

" ' I thought that was to your taste. You commonly hate much volubility. How have I heard you bemoan yourself when attacked by Miss Larolles !'

" ' Larolles!—oh, distraction! She talks me into a fever in two minutes. But so it is for ever.

Nothing but extremes to be met with! Common
girls are too forward, this lady is too reserved—
always some fault! Always some drawback!
Nothing ever perfect!'

" ' Nay, nay!' cried Mr. Gosport—'you do not
know her; she is perfect enough, in all conscience.'

" ' Better not know her, then,' answered he,
again yawning, 'for she cannot be pleasing.
Nothing perfect is natural—I hate everything out
of nature.' "

Captain Aresby is a universal lover, whose
admiration has no value, and Mr. Meadows, as an
ennuyé, is bound to care about no woman. Cecilia,
however, has three genuine lovers : Mr. Monckton,
a false friend, married to an old wife, and who,
whilst anxiously hoping for that lady's decease,
tries to save up Cecilia for himself—Mr. Arnold,
Mrs. Harrel's brother, a sincere and devoted lover,
whose affection Cecilia can only repay with esteem
—and Sir Robert Floyer, an insolent and surly
man, whom she detests. This gentleman's temper,
and the mode of wooing he is likely to adopt, are
well displayed in the remarks a first and staring
survey of the heiress suggests to him.

He is asked how he likes Harrel's ward—

" ' Why, faith, I don't know—but not much, I think. She's a devilish fine woman, too—but she has no spirit, no life.'

" ' Did you try her ? Have you talked to her ? '

" ' Not I, truly.'

" ' Nay, then, how do you mean to judge of her ? '

" ' Oh, faith, that's all over now; one never thinks of talking to the women by way of trying them.'

" ' What other method, then, have you adopted ? '

" ' None.'

" ' None ? Why, then, how do you go on ? '

" ' Why, they talk to us. The women take all that trouble upon themselves now.'

" ' And pray how long may you have commenced *fade macaroni?* For this is a part of your character with which I was not acquainted.'

" ' Oh, hang it, 'tis not from *ton;* no, it's merely from laziness. Who the d—l will fatigue himself with dancing attendance upon the women, when keeping them at a distance makes them dance attendance upon us ? ' "

Between this gentleman's insolence, supported
as he is by Mr. Harrel, who is in debt, and that
unworthy guardian's extravagance, Cecilia is put
into strange predicaments. Mr. Harrel cannot allow
so much living money as an heiress to be in his
house and not borrow, and, with a perfect contempt for him and his extravagance, Cecilia cannot
resist his importunities. An accommodating usurer
is found, the money is raised, and Miss Beverley,
with good sense, natural prudence, an invincible
dislike to debt and extravagance, and the best intentions of spending her handsome fortune in wise
or benevolent purposes, finds herself the abettor of
a confirmed and unscrupulous gambler.

Sir Robert Floyer is not less troublesome in his
way. Though doing nothing to ensure her esteem
or her liking, he considers Cecilia his own, and
fights a duel with a Mr. Belfield, whose escort
Miss Beverley preferred to his   This unfortunate
event introduces Cecilia to some new characters,
and to new perplexities. Mr. Belfield is a young
man of humble birth but good education, whom
his shame of his family, poverty, and irritable pride
render miserable. He is ill with the fever of the
wound he received in the duel, and during his

illness he is nursed by his sister, a sweet young
girl, and his mother, a vain, vulgar woman, admirably drawn. Cecilia is introduced to Miss Belfield by the man-hater; she visits her, and Mrs.
Belfield can account for these visits but one way—
Miss Beverley is in love with her son, but he is
unfortunately too shy, too shamefaced; Mrs. Belfield promises Cecilia that he will mend.

"But pray, now, ma'am, don't think him the
more ungrateful for his shyness, for young ladies
so high in the world as you are must go pretty
good lengths before a young man will get courage
to speak to them. And though I have told my
son, over and over, that the ladies never like a
man the worse for being a little bold, he's so much
down in the mouth that it has no effect upon him.
But it all comes of his being brought up at the
university, for that makes him think he knows
better than I can tell him. And so, to be sure, he
does. However, for all that, it is a hard thing
upon a mother to find all she says just goes for
nothing. But I hope you'll excuse him, ma'am,
for it's nothing in the world but his over-modesty."

In vain Cecilia looks amazed and displeased,
Mrs. Belfield's apologies are worse than the offence.

" ' We mothers of families,' she kindly says, ' are more used to speak out than maiden ladies.'

" 'Oh, dear, mother,' cried Miss Belfield, whose face was the colour of scarlet, ' pray—'

" ' What's the matter now ? ' cried Mrs. Belfield ; ' you are as shy as your brother, and if we are all to be so, when are we to come to an understanding ? '

" ' Not immediately, I believe, indeed,' said Cecilia, rising ; ' but that we may not plunge deeper in our mistakes, I will for the present take my leave.'

" ' Lack-a-day!' cried Mrs. Belfield, with scarcely smothered vexation, ' how hard it is to make these grand young ladies come to reason.' "

This character is exquisitely sustained. Nothing can remove Mrs. Belfield's conviction that Cecilia is in love with her son, and that she might just as well know her own mind once for all, and marry him.

" To be sure, any lady that knew her own true advantage could do nothing better than to take the recommendation of a mother, who must naturally know more of her own children's disposition than can be expected from a stranger ; and as to

such a son as mine, perhaps there arn't two such
in the world, for he's had a gentleman's education,
and, turn him which way he will, he'll see never a
handsomer person than his own; though, my
poor dear love, he was always of the thinnest. But
the misfortunes he's had to struggle with would
make nobody fatter."

And coldly though Cecilia listens to such hints,
and to the advice of marrying for love some one
who will take care of her and her fortune, the unwearied mother yet exclaims, as Miss Beverley
takes her departure :

" Lack-a-day, ma'am, I hope you won't go yet,
for I expect my son home soon, and I've a heap of
things to talk to you about besides; only Mr.
Hobson having so much to say stopt my mouth.
But I should take it as a great favour, ma'am, if
you would come some afternoon and drink a dish
of tea with me, for then we should have time to
say all our say. And I'm sure, ma'am, if you
would only let one of your footmen just take a
run to let me know when you'd come, my son
would be very proud to give you the meeting ; and
the servants can't have much else to do at your
house, for, where there's a heap of 'em, they

commonly think of nothing all day long but standing and gaping at one another."

No less admirably portrayed are Mr. and Mrs.
Harrel, though too culpable to be entertaining.
Cecilia has raised £600; £400 have gone to Mr.
Harrel, who, seized with an irresistible longing for
the remaining £200, gets hold of them, spite all
Cecilia's reluctance.   In vain Miss Beverley
remonstrates.   Mr. Harrel makes promises he
does not keep; and Mrs. Harrel, horrified at the
prospect of reform and economy, and evidently
considering both no better than perdition, coolly
asks what worse can happen when they are ruined?

This catastrophe is soon impending.   Creditors
threaten an execution, Mrs. Harrel locks herself
up, and Cecilia is left alone with Mr. Harrel, who
takes hold of a razor, and, with a frenzy half-real,
half-acted, vows he will not survive his ruin and
disgrace.   Cecilia, distracted with terror, and
indignant though compassionate, swears to pay
Mr. Harrel's debts, and parts with £7,500.   A
grand rout, given to convince the fashionable
world that the Harrels were never more affluent,
proves to Miss Beverley how hopeless is their
reformation.

And yet, against her better judgment she is again drawn in. With such perfect skill is all this told, that we feel flight alone could save Cecilia's purse. Mr. Harrel comes home a fierce and ruined man. He has contracted a debt of honour, which he cannot pay—he is disgraced, and must fly. His fury is vented on his wife. To save her early friend from ill-usage and assist their flight, the distracted, though reluctant, Cecilia is again importuned out of a thousand pounds.

And now, robbed of almost the whole of her paternal fortune of ten thousand pounds, she thinks to take refuge in Mr. Delvile's house, when a last strange request is preferred. Mr. Harrel has consented to leave his wife behind him, but he insists on parting from her in Vauxhall—and to Vauxhall the distressed Cecilia is persecuted in accompanying them.

All that follows is striking and impressive. We feel the union of the tragic and comic elements which has ever marked the great English school, from the days of Shakespeare downwards; that union, so foreign to the solemnity of the ancients and to the decorum of the moderns, but so con-

sistent with truth, so deep, so utterly melancholy
in its contrasts of mirth and gloom.   Miss Burney
must have possessed great natural dramatic power
to have related, as she did, these last dismal hours
of the ruined and dishonoured Mr. Harrel.   His
wild spirits prepare us for a catastrophe; and the
two duns, who discover and persecute him in
Vauxhall, and who finally sit down and sup with
him, add to the sense of calamity with which we
watch the progress of this strange evening.   Mr.
Hobson and Mr. Simpkins are the grotesque and
bitter spectres of Mr. Harrel's vices.   Even in this
last tragic scene of gaiety they haunt his steps and
inflict upon him the pangs of a last agony.

Mr. Hobson is fat, vulgar, well-fed, " with an air
of defiance that spoke the fulness of his purse."
He is a thorough man of business—he thinks all
places good for the settlement of a debt, and he
accosts Mr. Harrel, who answers him with a curse,
and threatens to break his bones, to which Mr.
Hobson logically replies—

" ' Sir, this is talking quite out of character; for
as to broken bones, there's ne'er a person in all
England, gentle nor simple, can say he's a right to
break mine, for I'm not a person of that sort, but

a man of as good property as another man; and there's ne'er a customer I have in the world that's more his own man than myself.' "

It is not in his position as a free man or as an injured creditor that Mr. Hobson rests his right not to have his bones broken; no, his purse is his justice, his law, his freedom, even as it is his soul and his God. Rancorous he is not, however, for he accepts Mr. Harrel's flighty invitations to supper; he is soon as merry as his host, and when Sir Robert Floyer, coming up to them surlily, asks, " Who the devil Mr. Harrel has picked up ?" Mr. Hobson, who, to the importance of lately acquired wealth, now added the courage of newly drunk champagne, stoutly kept his ground, without seeming at all conscious he was included in this interrogation; but Mr. Simpkins, who had still his way to make in the world, and whose habitual servility would have resisted a larger draught, was easily intimidated; he again, therefore, stood up, and with the most cringing respect offered the Baronet his place, who, taking neither of the offer nor offerer the smallest notice, still stood opposite to Mr. Harrel, waiting for some explanation.

Mr. Harrel, however, who now grew really

incapable of giving any, only repeated his invitation, that he would make one among them."

"One among you!" cried he, angrily, and
pointing to Mr. Hobson; "why, you don't fancy
I'll sit down with a bricklayer?"

"A bricklayer?" said Mr. Harrel, "ay, sure,
and a hosier too; sit down, Mr. Simpkins, keep
your place, man."

Mr. Simpkins most thankfully bowed; but Mr.
Hobson, who could no longer avoid feeling the
personality of this reflection, boldly answered,
"Sir, you may sit down with a worse man any
day in the week! I have done nothing I'm
ashamed of, and no man can say to me, 'Why did
you so?' I don't tell you, sir, what I'm worth;
no one has a right to ask. I only say, three
times five is fifteen, that's all."

In short, Mr. Hobson is a man of substance,
and, to use his own significant words, "not to be
treated like a little scrubby apprentice."

This dismal entertainment ends with the foreseen catastrophe: Mr. Harrel kisses his wife,
rushes away and blows his brains out. Cecilia's
thousand pounds given for the journey had been
risked on one stake and lost at the gambling house.

The connection with the Harrels ending thus tragically, Delvile Castle now becomes Miss Beverley's home. Welcome is the change ; for, if her guardian is formal and pompous, Mrs. Delvile, though proud, unites sweetness and dignity with her pride; and Mortimer Delvile, elegant, amiable, and accomplished, is all that even a Cecilia can dream of. Chance has made her and this young man meet often, never without mutually discovering new perfections on either side. A supposed partiality for young Belfield, and then an imaginary promise to Sir Robert Floyer, seemed alone to prevent Mortimer Delvile's assiduities from melting into tenderness. Cecilia's heart is his, this she knows, and she cannot but think her secret fondness returned. She knows, too, that her handsome fortune would be acceptable to this impoverished though noble, family ; and her birth, though not distinguished, is not so mean as to be an obstacle. Yet no sooner is she under the same roof with him than she is carefully shunned by her guardian's son. Through all this coldness appear sudden bursts of tenderness, which convince her that she is beloved. Mrs. Delvile, from whose piercing eyes nothing is hidden, gives Cecilia to understand that her beauty, virtue, accomplishments, and large fortune would be all the heir of the Delviles could wish for, if it were possible for the last of that noble race to assume the name of Beverley.

Grieved, but too much hurt in her pride to be heartbroken, Cecilia returns to Suffolk. And now we come to the weakest passages in the book—the love passages. Manners and characters, perplexities of incident, were Miss Burney's *forte;* when passion developed character, when pride and will were in contest, she excelled, but the subtle graces of tenderness, of those vague feelings which scarcely know how to leave the heart, she knew not how to deal with.

A mischievous young lady, a cousin of Mr. Delvile's, has stolen and sent Cecilia Mortimer's dog Fidèle. That Miss Beverley should love and cherish it for its master's sake is true to nature, but that she, a prudent and dignified young lady, should, sitting in a garden, utter aloud to that animal a confession of her tenderness for his master, is a painful absurdity, all the more painful from the exquisite exactness and truth of Miss Burney's general painting.

The confession is overheard by Delvile, come
down to Suffolk on a suspicion of its truth;
and in his transport, for he had only suspected his
happiness, he proposes a secret marriage; Cecilia is
shocked, startled, and finally she consents. She is
of age now, and her own mistress; but Mr. Monckton, in whom she confides, alarmed at the risk he
runs, so forcibly shows her the loss of dignity she
will suffer by this stealthy and indelicate proceeding, that he persuades her to retract, and though
she journeys to town to meet her lover, as had
been agreed, it is to soften the blow of his disappointment — not to fulfil her promise. But a
lover's arguments, enforced by his presence and
tender entreaties, prevail over better judgment. A
licence has been procured, the clergyman is waiting. Cecilia, Mrs. Charlton her friend, and Delvile proceed to —— Church, where the ceremony
begins. A very dramatic incident follows:

"Cecilia, finding herself past all power of re-
tracting, soon called her thoughts from wish-
ing it, and turned her whole attention to the awful service; to which, though she listened with
reverence, her full satisfaction in the object of her
vows made her listen without terror. But when

the priest came to that solemn adjuration, '*If any
man can shew any just cause why they may not be
lawfully joined together,*' a conscious tear stole into
her eye, and a sigh escaped from Delvile that went
to her heart; but when the priest concluded the ex-
hortation with, '*let him now speak, or else hereafter
for ever hold his peace,*' a female voice at some
distance called out in shrill accents, ' I do ! '

" The ceremony was instantly stopped. The
astonished priest immediately shut up the book to
regard the intended bride and bridegroom; Delvile started with amazement to see whence the
sound proceeded, and Cecilia, aghast, and struck
with horror, faintly shrieked, and caught hold of
Mrs. Charlton."

The person who thus interrupted the ceremony
is not discovered, but the effect is produced on
Cecilia's mind.   Shocked and hurt, she returns
unmarried to Suffolk ; here a visit from Mrs. Delvile, who knows all, and who works on Miss Beverley's pride and feelings, produces a formal renun-
ciation of Delvile.   He is brought to hear his fate
decided, but, by refusing to acquiesce in it, so rouses
all his haughty mother's passions, that she bursts
a bloodvessel.   Her life is in danger—in the hour

of grief all resistance vanishes—Cecilia and Delvile
part with the solemn engagement to meet no more
without her consent.

Although Miss Burney's peculiar excellence lay
in the painting of strongly marked vulgarity, she
was certainly very successful in the proud, dignified, sweet, and yet haughty Mrs. Delvile. The
skill and power with which she pursues her end,
the sincerity that redeems her pride, the high honour that seems to justify it, interest us in her favour, even whilst she is bent on making Cecilia,
whom she loves, and her son, whom she adores,
wretched for life. We have already said that
Miss Burney had a gift for painting the small perplexities which make up the life of many a woman; but
though the complications that bring us to the close
of this well-wrought story are interesting, they
too often fail in probability to produce a lasting
impression on the mind.

Cecilia is of age; she comes to town to release
her guardians, and she finds Mr. Delvile not
merely irritated on account of the passion which
had led his son to the verge of disobedience, but
strangely prejudiced against her. He attributes
to her a passion for young Belfield, and for his

sake he is convinced that she had dealings with a
money-lender, and spent the best part of her ten
thousand pounds. Denial does not shake this
impression, and as he applies for imformation to
Mrs. Belfield, Cecilia, who happens to be with
Miss Belfield in the next room, has the satisfaction
of hearing that lady confirm her secret passion for
her son. The scene is excellent.

"'I am sure, sir, I shall be very willing to
oblige you,' Mrs. Belfield answered; 'but pray,
sir, what's your name?'

"'My name, ma'am,' he replied, in a rather
elevated voice; 'I am seldom obliged to announce
myself; nor is there any present necessity I should
make it known. It is sufficient I assure you, you
are speaking to no very common person, and probably to one you will have little chance to meet
with again.'

"'But how can I tell your business, sir, if I
don't so much as know your name?'

"'My business, ma'am, I mean to tell myself;
your affair is only to hear it. I have some questions, indeed, to ask, which I must trouble you to
answer, but they will sufficiently explain themselves to prevent any difficulty upon your part.

There is no need, therefore, of any introductory ceremonial.'

" ' Well, sir,' said Mrs. Belfield, wholly insensible of this ambiguous greatness, 'if you mean to make your name a secret——'

" ' Few names, I believe, ma'am,' cried he, haughtily, ' have less the advantage of secrecy than mine. On the contrary, this is but one among a very few houses in this town to which my person would not immediately announce it. That, however, is immaterial, and you will be so good as to rest satisfied with my assurances that the person with whom you are now conversing will prove no disgrace to your character.' "

After this pompous introduction, Mr. Delvile condescends to come to the point. Has Mr. Belfield made any proposals to a young lady of fortune?

" ' Lack-a-day, no, sir,' answered Mrs. Belfield, to the infinite relief of Cecilia, who instantly concluded this question referred to herself.

" ' I beg your pardon, then; good morning to you, ma'am,' said Mr. Delvile, in a tone that spoke his disappointment; but added, 'and there is no such young person, you say, who favours his pretensions?'

"'Dear sir,' cried she, 'why, there's nobody he'll so much as put the question to; there's a young lady at this very time, a great fortune, that has as much mind to him, I tell him, as any man need desire to see; but there's no making him think it, though he has been brought up at the university, and knows more about all the things, or as much as anybody in the king's dominions.'

"'Oh! then,' cried Mr. Delvile, in a voice of far more complacency, 'it is not on the side of the young woman that the difficulty seems to rest?'

"'Lord, no, sir, he might have had her again and again, only for asking. She came after him ever so often . . . . . she found him out, sir, when not one of his own natural friends could tell where in the world he was gone. She was the first, sir, to come and tell me news of him, though I was his own mother. Love, sir, is pro- digious for quickness; it can see, I sometimes think, through bricks and mortar. Yet all this would not do, he was so obstinate not to take the hint.'"

Mr. Delvile's swelling exultation at these con- fessions is, however, short-lived.

"'And as to young ladies themselves,' continued

Mrs. Belfield, ' they know no more how to make
their minds known than a baby does ; so I suppose
he'll shilly-shally till somebody else will cry snap,
and take her. It is but a little while ago that it
was all the report she was to have young Mr. Delvile, one of her guardian's sons.'

" ' I am sorry report was so impertinent,' cried
Mr. Delvile, with much displeasure ; ' young Mr.
Delvile is not to be disposed of with so little
ceremony—he knows better what is due to his
family.'

" ' Lord, sir,' answered Mrs. Belfield, ' what
should his family do better ? I never heard they
were any so rich, and I dare say the old gentleman, being her guardian, took care to put his
son enough in her way ; however, it came about
that they did not make a match of it, for, as to old
Mr. Delvile, all the world says '——

" ' All the world takes a very great liberty,' angrily interrupted Mr. Delvile, ' in saying anything
about him ; and you will excuse my informing you
that a person of his rank and consideration is not
lightly to be mentioned upon every little occasion
that occurs.'

" ' Lord, sir,' cried Mrs. Belfield, somewhat surprized at this unexpected prohibition, 'I don't care, for my part, if I never mention the old gentleman's name again! I never heard any good of him in my life, for they say he's as proud as Lucifer, and nobody knows what it's of; for they say '——

"'They say,' cried he, firing with rage, 'and who are they? Be so good as inform me that?'

"'Lord, everybody, sir! it's his common character.'

"'Then everybody is extremely indecent,' speaking very loud, 'to pay no more respect to one of the first families in the land. It is a licentiousness that ought by no means to be suffered with impunity.'"

Cecilia is discovered in the next room, and Mr. Delvile departs insolent and triumphant.

The tale ends happily, however, in spite of him, but that happy end is not felicitously produced. Mrs. Delvile relents, and proposes that Cecilia shall forfeit her estate and marry Mortimer, who cannot assume her name. Cecilia consents; the marriage takes place privately, without Mr. Delvile's consent or knowledge. When the marriage is over, Mrs. Delvile and her son prepare to depart for the Continent, for the restoration of that lady's health, and

Cecilia returns to Suffolk. There she is soon convinced that Mr. Monckton had betrayed and slandered her to Mr. Delvile, and bribed his wife's companion to interrupt the ceremony of her secret marriage, which she had confided to him. Scarcely had she made this discovery when she learns that her husband has wounded Mr. Monckton in a duel. He flies, leaving her a prey to fears, on which worldly anxieties soon follow. Her marriage is known, and the house and estate she has forfeited are claimed by the next heirs. She hastens to London, to be distracted by her husband's jealousy of Belfield, with whom he seems ready for another fatal duel, and to be refused an asylum in the house of her haughty father-in-law. Reason forsakes her as she wanders, at night, about the streets of London raving mad and calling on her husband.

She is taken in by a pawnbroker, discovered by her friends, and finally restored to health; every wound is healed, every wrong is forgotten, and everything is made right, save that the estate is lost, and that Cecilia ceases to be an " heiress."

The madness of Cecilia is painful and unnatural. This amiable but self-possessed lady could

not go mad thus without warning. But Dr.
Lyster will tell us the object this fit of insanity
was to answer.

"Thus, my dear young lady, the terror which
drove you to this house, and the sufferings which
have confined you in it, will prove, in the event,
the source of your future peace; for, when all my
best rhetoric failed to melt Mr. Delvile, I instantly
brought him to terms by coupling his name with
a pawnbroker's! And he could not with more
disgust hear his son called Mr. Beverley than think
of his son's wife when he hears of the *Three Blue
Balls!*"

Miss Burney wrote but four novels. Improvement as she progressed was not, however, her lot.
The merits of "Evelina" and "Cecilia" are well-
nigh equal, but "Camilla" was a falling off, and
"The Wanderer" was a failure. In both, in
Camilla especially, we find the remains of great
talent, of character, liveliness, and power; but the
contrast between them and their predecessors is
striking. In both we again perceive how sorely
Miss Burney was troubled with the perplexities
which attend the lot of woman in the world; how

anxious she felt concerning the prudence, reserve, and caution which should guide her least actions. It is curious to contrast her novels with those of her cotemporary, Madame de Staël. Delphine dies a victim to the worldly prejudices of her lover—Corinne is sacrificed to society and its fears; but even though we may censure both Delphine and Corinne, our sympathies are in their favour, and the teaching of the tale is that genius, independence, and generous feelings ought not to be so strictly fettered by social laws. Miss Burney takes no such flight. Her heroines are amiable, correct, and good; but so inexorable is she to the least dereliction from the right path of prudence—for virtue is never questioned—that she is ready to inflict every sorrow and every humiliation upon them if they take a step beyond its narrow limits. The world is right, and always right—if they suffer, let them thank their own folly for their sorrows.

The troubles of Camilla are not so entertaining, however, as those of young Evelina or of the amiable Cecilia. She is a light, airy, poor and imprudent, but gentle girl. Her lover, Edgar, is a prudent, rich, and wise young man. Camilla

trusts too much, and Edgar too little. His caution
is fortified by a twice-disappointed widower, whose
experience assures him that youth, beauty, and
the most amiable qualities in a wife are not sufficient to secure a husband's happiness—her affection must be disinterested, else both are undone.
Now, Camilla, a clergyman's daughter, with three
sisters, one brother, and no portion, may not be
quite disinterested. She may even marry Edgar,
not exactly for his money, but without love.
Prudence requires that the owner of a noble
estate should not surrender blindly to her power.

Thanks to this painful wisdom, Edgar and
Camilla are miserable through five volumes.
They have every opportunity, yet can never come
to a fair understanding. When they are actually
betrothed, fate perversely parts them, apparently
for ever.

No doubt Camilla is imprudent, and no doubt
Edgar is hasty in his conclusions, but the opposition in their tempers is not so great as to justify
a result so violent. The point is strained, that
both may be punished, and from that moment the
story loses much in interest and truth. But one
thing it never can lose—the author's wonderful

skill in painting manners and peculiarities. In
Camilla she has chosen to fetter herself with
various young people, some of whom are not very
interesting, and who interfere unduly; but admirable she is always when she takes a wider range.
The old uncle of Camilla is a charming character.
Vehement and simple as a child—ignorant, and
attributing all his mistakes to that unfortunate
want of Greek and Latin, the result of an idle
youth, he is the kindest-hearted and most injudicious of men. Especially delightful is his innocence; it invests him with a delicacy which
creates veneration. His goodness might be the
result of a warm heart, but his ingenuous ignorance of evil has something sacred and child-like;
whilst the pertinacity with which he considers
every blunder the result of book ignorance, and
every good or courageous act of book knowledge,
is as provoking as his strange fancy for match-
making.

This amiable old gentleman is surrounded by
young people, whom he mates for the best, but
whose perversity ruins all his fondest plans. His
plain niece, whom he has made a classic scholar,
is despised by the poor and insolent cousin to whom

she was destined ; his handsome niece is not more
acceptable to Edgar, and Camilla, who was to stay
with him, chooses to fall in love with the very man
her cousin was to marry. Yet of all this the kind
uncle long remains ignorant. Young people grow
enamoured, quarrel, and are reconciled under his
very eyes, and he sees it not, or, seeing it, does not
understand. Whilst they are progressing on the
journey of love he wanders in an imaginary land,
in which everything comes to pass as he has plan-
ned it, and rude and harsh are the many waken-
ings he gets on the way ; harshest of all is the final
one, when a series of unplanned marriages, two of
them runaway matches, close his matrimonial
campaign.

Of all the faculties which contribute to the
pleasure a work of fiction can yield, there is none
more precious than vivacity. It is amazing how
many deficiencies this one excellence will cover.
Its charm, indeed, is that it bears us on, and makes
us forget all else. The greatest faults of a story
are not heeded when the narrative is lively. But
when, on the contrary, age, sorrow, and the serious-
ness of experience have dispelled this early fascina-
tion, when the narrator sits down and tells us in

sober guise a story which should be invested with all the keen vivacity of early days, it is in vain that characters are well conceived, incidents strongly cast, and a mystery well kept up; dulness—woful dulness—opens the first page, and closes the last; and the harsh, but not unjust, sentence, that the writer has exhausted his power to please, must be pronounced.

Some such sentence must certainly have been recorded against Madame d'Arblay's last novel, "The Wanderer; or Female Difficulties." There is much of her peculiar merit in it, but little or none of her peculiar charm. That liveliness which outlived in her the first season of youth, could not reach the dawn of age. The "Wanderer" is a dull story in spite of character, incident, evident care and minor merits. Yet we think that many circumstances, more than failure of power, contributed to its want of success.

It was begun at the close of the last century, finished in 1814, and written during a critical turning-point of taste. It bears witness to the uncertainty of the writer's mind. A composition extended over so long a period, and carried on with the consciousness that a more impassioned and romantic school was beginning to prevail, could not but lose in concentration and power. Madame d'Arblay, struck with the tendency of such works as "Delphine" for instance, painted in good earnest the character of a sceptical, impassioned woman, who makes herself ridiculous without ever being entertaining. The attempt to engraft this, and scenes and incidents of similar character, all so foreign to her Johnsonian mind, on that ever favourite theme, "female difficulties," was awkward, ill-judged, and lamentable in its results.

The story of "The Wanderer" was chosen and conducted with reference to those feminine troubles which from first to last Miss Burney and Madame d'Arblay held to be the great troubles of life. It is remarkable that the sorrows of her heroines never spring from within. It is not temper, pride, passion, or folly that leads them into mischief or misery. This is one of the points in which Miss Burney is so inferior to her contemporaries, Miss Edgeworth and Mrs. Inchbald. They knew where the springs of life lie hidden. With Miss Burney the evil is always external, social, worldly, the offspring of manners, circumstance, fortune, or birth. Involuntary concealment of name and parentage, the condition of a will, vulgar or injudicious relations, do all the mischief—it is always small or mean in its nature, though potent in its effects. The cause is here kept a mystery till the end. We see the troubles, but do not know whence they spring, and what could remove them.

A party of English travellers leave France during the Reign of Terror. It is a dark December night, the vessel is ready to sail, when a woman's voice is heard from the shore passionately entreating to be received on board. Her request is granted after much doubt and hesitation, and the traveller, clad in mean attire, dark as a berry, covered with bandages and patches, is very coarsely received by the party to which she has introduced herself. She neither heeds jests nor answers questions, but seems absorbed in the ecstatic joy of escape. This joy is sobered when on landing she discovers that her purse is gone, and that she stands penniless on a shore which, though not foreign—for she is English—does not prove very hospitable.

The difficulties of the wanderer begin ; she has no money, she claims no friends, she proves to be

young and beautiful, for the dark complexion was
a wash, and the patches and bandages were mere
disguise, everything, in short, proves her to be
an adventurer and an impostor. The necessities
of a fantastic traveller, Mrs. Ireton, convey her
to London, and the caprice of a young lady, Miss
Joddrell, helps her on to Lewes. She is even
admitted into the family of that young lady's aunt,
Mrs. Maple; her beauty, her accomplishments,
fascinate all who do not know her story, and
secure the love of Mr. Harleigh, who does. She
returns his affection ; we see and know it, but she
will not tell him who she is. In vain every species
of perplexity and mortification await her—in vain
she is humbled, insulted, and persecuted—she
keeps her secret. An imprudent word, she says,
can ruin her ; what that word is we do not know.
We are not told what Harleigh's ardent prayers
failed to win, but though there is a species of
interest in this mystery, it is a tedious one, and is
not revealed till the end of the tale.

Juliet Granville is the daughter of an English
nobleman by a secret marriage. She is reared
in France by kind friends, and disowned by Lord
Denmeath, the guardian of her young brother

and sister. The documents relating to her birth
are burnt in the château of her friends. A pro-
missory note of 6,000*l*., payable on her marriage
with a Frenchman, the only concession Lord Denmeath has made to her rights, falls, however, into
the hands of a commissary of the Republic.
Lured by such a prize, he makes Juliet's hand
the price of the life of one of her kind protectors.
They are hastily united, her lips utter no vows,
the marriage is marriage enough to bind her in
honour, but not to make her stay with so debased
a wretch. She flies to England, and this is her
secret. She keeps it well, yet he discovers her,
pursues her, and claims her. The alien bill inter-
feres and saves her, and his death delivers her
finally, and restores her to liberty, love, and social
rank.

"The Wanderer" was a failure, and did not
deserve success. It was, and wisely, Madame
d'Arblay's last novel. "Evelina" and "Cecilia"
were celebrated in their day, and their charm has
not departed with the manners they painted.
They still give us striking and interesting pictures
of English society during the last twenty-five
years of the eighteenth century. In one very

characteristic feature they agree with Miss Edge-worth's delineations of the fashionable world in the first years of the present age. The coarse-ness and insolence of men who then moved in the polite world are such as may now surprise us. Either society is more polished, or women have learned to soften their representation of its aspects. The truth probably lies between either fact. The feminine element in both these great novelists is shown in the reserve and delicacy with which they treat love; but the womanly picture of society, as it is now practised, they were too free, and perhaps too frank, to conceive. With them there is no softening touch, no grace, given to insolence, coarseness, and pride. Their being women only seems to make them more resentful of what is always more or less an insult to woman's power; and no scruple saved a Mr. Smith, a Sir Robert Floyer, or a Sir Philip Baddeley from unmerciful but just castigation.

CHAPTER VII.

MRS. CHARLOTTE SMITH.

THERE are lives that read like one long sorrow, and that leave little save sadness and disappointment behind them when they close in death. Such a life was that of Charlotte Smith, full of cares while it lasted, and, once it was over, doomed to fade away from memory. She had great talent—she was one of the best novelists of the day, but the haste and facility with which she wrote, the gloom that overshadowed her life, robbed her of a durable literary fame. As a poetess she is forgotten; as a novelist she but helps to fill the vacant space between Miss Burney and Mrs. Radcliffe. She partakes of the power of these two remarkable women, but only in an inferior degree.

She has not the vigour of the one, or the picturesque faculty of the other. Yet she, too, could
draw character—witness Mrs. Rayland in the
"Old Manor House"—and she, too, could paint
the aspect of nature, as many a clear, fresh landscape in the same novel proves. To hold a place
in that middle region is great good fortune for the
living, but for the dead it is little; and if we
attempt to give Charlotte Smith her meed of praise
in these pages, it is not without the knowledge
that she produced no strong impression, and will
leave no lasting trace in the literature of her
country.

Charlotte Turner, daughter of Nicholas Turner,
of Stoke House, Surrey, and Bignor Park, Sussex,
was born in London, on the 4th of May, 1749.
She was only four years old when her mother
died, and she was confided to the care of an
aunt. She was put to school in Kensington, then
a fashionable place for education, but she was considered too great a genius to study. She learned a
few accomplishments—was eminent in dancing, could
draw, acted with great effect in school theatricals,
and left, at the ripe age of twelve, to enter into
the gaieties of a London life. At fourteen she re-

ceived an offer of marriage, which her father declined; and, at fifteen, she contracted that unfortunate union which, without giving her husband
happiness, was to her a long source of misery.

Mr. Turner had been ten years a widower when
he thought of marrying again. Charlotte's aunt,
alarmed at the prospect of a stepmother for her
favourite, found no better remedy for the future
evil than the present dangerous risk of a husband.
A Mr. Smith, aged twenty-one, was found and
prepared to fall in love with her niece, who also
received the injunction to welcome his passion;
the young people proved docile; and in February,
1765, Miss Turner was married. Mr. Smith's
father was a West India merchant, and a Direc-
tor of the East India Company. The home and
the family to which a young, romantic, and accomplished girl found herself introduced, were
enough to chill any bride's heart. A house in one
of the narrowest and dirtiest lanes in the City, and
in which the sun's beams had never shone, was
her abode; a sickly, languid mother-in-law—tall,
thin, and murmuring—a notable West Indian
housewife, ever complaining of English young
ladies' ways, was her daily society. A keen-eyed

father-in-law—a thorough City man—a contemner of fashionable accomplishments, and the sound of whose creaking shoes was enough to make young Mrs. Smith hide up whatever she might be doing, was her privileged censor. Yet either was better than her foolish, ignorant, pleasure-seeking, and dissipated husband. Ill-health gave Mrs. Smith a plea for a change. She went to Southgate, and managed to live no more with old Mr. Smith, who, after his wife's death, married her aunt, to whose zeal she was indebted for her unenviable position.

The death of her father-in-law proved the first of a series of disasters for Mrs. Charlotte Smith. Mr. Smith had made his will himself, and drawn it up so badly as to involve his whole family in contests. The complications of business, law, and perversity, which brought Mrs. Smith's husband to a prison, are not very interesting, but from the days when she shared his confinement, to her own death, in 1806, her life was a succession of cares, with few respites. After remaining in prison with her husband for seven months, she went, on his release, to Sussex, where her children had stayed during that dreary time. "After the scenes I had witnessed, and the apprehensions I had suffered," she

says herself, "how deliciously soothing to my
wearied spirits was the soft pure air of the summer's morning, breathing over the dewy grass, as
we passed over the Surrey heaths. My native hills
at length burst upon my view; I beheld once more
the fields where I had passed my happiest days, and
amidst the perfumed turf with which one of those
fields was strewn, perceived with delight the beloved group from whom I had been so long divided,
and for whose fate my affections were ever anxious. The transports of this meeting were too much
for my exhausted spirits; yet, after all my sufferings, I began to hope I might taste content, or
experience at least a respite from calamity." Never
was hope more signally disappointed; poverty and
its cares, the deaths of beloved children, the struggles of a literary career, domestic unhappiness,
which, in 1785, after a union of ten years, ended
in separation, such was her destiny—a sad one in
its brightest and earliest days, if we except those
of childhood.

It was in 1788, a few years after the appearance
of "Cecilia," which the heroine is represented as
reading, that Mrs. Smith published her first novel,
"Emmeline, or the Orphan of the Castle." It

was extremely successful. " Ethelinda " followed the next year, and " Celestina " in 1791. Then came a political novel ; for Mrs. Smith was, like Mrs. Inchbald, a partisan of the new doctrines of the day, and, like her, she lived in the intimacy of many fiery spirits of those exciting times. " Desmond," and " The Old Manor House," her best novels, poems and other productions, original tales and translations, kept her for nearly twenty years before the public. Her mind was quick and lively ; she never remembered learning how to read, and she wrote with great facility. Her father-in-law, having been slandered, asked her to refute the calumny for him, and was amazed at the rapidity with which she executed her task. Convinced that she would make a much better clerk than any he had, he offered her a considerable allowance for her services. This was before her literary days, but Mrs. Smith declined the proposal, and preferred liberty, till necessity compelled her to write. She liked the task, but the successive deaths of her children, who only reached man and woman's estate to be taken away before her eyes, broke her heart. Her daughter, who had married a French refugee, died in 1794, and though Mrs.

Smith survived her twelve years she never recovered the blow.

She said herself "Till the loss of my beloved
child, which fell upon me like the hand of death,
I could exert my faculties." At length her weary
life closed, on the 28th of October, 1806, at Til-
ford, where she resided, that she might be laid to
rest near her mother at Stoke. Mr. Smith, from
whom she had been separated twenty years, had
died in the preceding month of March. We
know little of Mrs. Smith, save what a few of her
friends have told us, yet there is no reason to
doubt their account of her faults and virtues. A
hasty temper, rendered irritable and resentful by
many trials, was her failing. Her works bear the
traces of asperity; but a generous devotedness to
those whom she loved, great charity to the poor, a
lively, cheerful disposition, and much fortitude to
endure, were her noble and redeeming traits. To
poetry she had always been addicted, but bitter
necessity made her a novelist.

CHAPTER VIII.

EMMELINE.—ETHELINDA.—THE OLD MANOR
HOUSE.

MRS. CHARLOTTE SMITH enjoyed a combination of
powers which rarely fail to acquire for their owner
a present reputation, and seldom secure a lasting
fame. She knew how to tell a story, and make it
interesting; she could sketch character with shrewd-
ness and truth ; she had feeling, and selected her
affecting incidents with judgment; her eye for
nature was true, and her descriptions were always
fresh, vivid, and natural. But she possessed not one
of these gifts in its fulness. It is not moderation,
but excess that strikes the public, and even posterity. Miss Burney verged on caricature, yet she
holds a far higher place than Mrs. Smith; Mrs.
Radcliffe was natural in nothing, her terror, her

landscapes, are utterly beyond all truth, yet she can still charm the imagination and win forgiveness for her sins. It is Mrs. Smith's fault that she has none, and yet is not perfect. Her best stories are tinged with a sort of mediocrity, which often looks like the effect of haste, and suggests that her powers were never fairly developed. It is hard to think that she who kept so clear from romantic folly and worldly coldness, who could paint pleasing and natural characters, and sketch such fresh and charming landscapes, could not have done better under more favourable circumstances. Even as it is, the place she holds in English literature is worthy of a record. She is a connecting link between opposite schools, and the most characteristic representative of the modern domestic novel. She is quite distinct in this respect from the writers of her times, and the combination, though in an inferior degree, of merits so different, is her claim to originality. She wrote much, and with unequal success. " Emmeline," " Ethelinda," and " The Old Manor House" are three of her best and most agreeable works. They are fully sufficient to shew us the bent and strength of her mind in fiction.

In " Emmeline " we have the graceful story of
an orphan girl pining under the stigma of illegiti-
mate birth and the miseries of dependance.   The
course of events at length restores her to her genuine
rank, and her long alienated inheritance, and makes
her happy with the man she loves, after many trials,
brought on by the circumstances of her position,
and the impetuosity of a man whose passion she
pities, but never shares.   Neither the story nor
the characters show much vigour, the incidents are
often utterly improbable, as, for instance, the manner in which the legitimacy of Emmeline's birth
remains so long undiscovered. The cast of the tale,
moreover, belongs to a school that never was good
—the school of distressed maidens, missing fathers,
children changed at nurse, &c.—a school to which
even the vivacious Evelina fell a victim ; but for all
that, " Emmeline " has many pleasing and tender
passages we could find in no other writer of the
times.

In " The Old Manor House" Orlando, the hero,
is the interesting character, but in " Emmeline,"
as in " Ethelinda," the heroine it is who wins and
attracts.   Of all the inevitable and natural results
brought on by the share women have had in writ-

ing novels, this is one which has most affected the
actual condition of woman in society. For a long
time men wrote alone, and their minds were the
minds of humanity. We had not the perfect and
twofold human being until women wrote. The
whole of literature was influenced by the change.
Delicacy, refinement, a pure moral and religious
tone, were its favourable results; the unfavourable
were and are the predominance given to love as
the great problem of human life, and an exaggeration of refinement that leads to social hypocrisy.
Effeminacy and falsehood are the two great increasing perils against which the literature of women must guard in England. These perils were
very slight at first, for all know in what state women found fiction — coarse and profane when it
was not licentious. The first aspect of its coarseness which revolted the female mind, was that which
is spoken. We find plenty of what we should call
coarseness now in the works of Miss Burney, Miss
Edgeworth even, Mrs. Opie, and Mrs. Inchbald. The adventures and dangers of the heroines
are not such as many women of our day would select
for delineation; but these young ladies, though not
sufficiently guarded from offence by the respect of

man and society, are, at least, modest in speech. If they often breathe an impure atmosphere, their language and their feelings are delicate. This was the first step, a great one, for with the progress of society the delicacy and reserve of women invariably extend to men.

But literature, especially English literature, where women came later than in France, had another aspect of coarseness besides that which was spoken; it had one which women of any refinement must by instinct have detested—the delineation of woman as mere woman—as the embodiment of beauty and the object of passion. The heroines of the early English novelists are all beautiful and virtuous; but their luxuriant beauty is far beyond their virtue. *This* is a matter of course, a social conventionalism, but without *that* they could not be heroines at all. They are not witty, they are not wise, they are not lofty or intellectual, they have none of the claims of real goodness or greatness; they are good-natured, often silly young creatures made to delight man, to amuse, tease, and obey him. Richardson, who lived in the society of the intellectual women of his age, who liked and respected women, knew best how to do them justice. His Clarissa is a great and noble creature. But not to speak of Smollett or Fielding, Goldsmith — the delicate, tender, and certainly refined Goldsmith — could not go beyond Sophia Primrose. She was his ideal of a heroine : a handsome, sensible, and quiet girl, capable of appreciating a superior man.

It is this undoubtedly coarse or low ideal of womanhood which women have displaced for ever. They have given their heroines virtue and beauty, but they have also given them something more. This change has been greatest in England, because in England it was that the long solitary progress of men in fiction made any contrast most remarkable. Mademoiselle de Scudéry enthroned the lofty, ideal, refined heroine; Madame de La Fayette showed us the woman of virtue—nobly resisting temptation, and of her struggles she made the subject of her longest and most charming novel; Madame de Tencin gave us the tender, impassioned woman ; Madame Riccoboni, the lovely, well-bred, lively, and generous lady of the *ancien régime.* Something between the *ancien régime* and the nineteenth century, are Madame de Genlis's heroines. Caliste, Amelie, Valérie, Delphine, and Corinne are more than mere *generic* heroines; they are beautiful and individual conceptions of character, some of the finest and the loftiest in the range of fiction.

Very distinct from these are the heroines of the female novelists of England. Aphra Behn's ideal of womanhood was coarse and low; Miss Fielding's was uncertain; like her brother, she dealt more with the humours of human nature than with its secret springs. Miss Burney's women indicate the great change, not that they are very remarkable, but they are something. Evelina's fortunes make the tale; her faults, her attractions, help out its incidents. Instead of standing in the background, a lovely young creature, ready to be wooed and won, she is a prominent figure, and acts a leading part from first to last. Cecilia is a still more important person. She is an heiress—she is cheated out of her money, persecuted and admired; and whatever befalls her, we feel that Miss Beverley is some one in society. Mrs. Smith's heroines are of another sort; they are generally poor, and in depressed circumstances; their importance is not that of birth, wealth, or fashion—it is that of intellect and refined manners.

They are ladies—young ladies, and the most perfect prototype of the lady in the modern novels of to-day. Emmeline is a gentle and sensitive girl, who likes to read by the sea-shore, or on the banks of quiet lakes. We feel the spirit of Thomson, of Gray, and Cowper in the tranquil scenes where she likes to move. She is beautiful, but beauty is her least attraction. She is thoughtful, amiable, modest, and intellectual; such a girl as any wise man would wish to marry. She is one of those women whose mental superiority over the less read and more active men of the same rank so struck Madame de Genlis, when she visited England, towards 1782, that she prophesied the days were not far off when the women of that country would acquire a high rank, and in some respects supremacy in literature. Her prophecy has, in some measure, been fulfilled, and it is impossible to over-estimate the effects of its accomplishment.

Novels have a double character—they reflect an age, and they influence it. They are a mirror and a model; and it is hard to say when one ceases and the other begins. Novels or romances —and what substantial difference is there between

them ?—are ideal, coarse, real or refined, as are
their authors and readers ; and the faults or virtues
which they image they have the great and often
dangerous power to magnify. It is impossible, for
instance, to conceive coarse books written in a
refined age, or refined books not helping to check
coarseness. This double action of literature leads
to some curious results. A tone of scepticism
or passion is often caught from a popular novel,
and influences a whole human destiny. An arti-
ficial passion for scenery is created, and men and
women who would otherwise have stayed quietly
at home are sent wandering, because they have
read certain books. The very nature of love, in-
asmuch as it partakes of the imagination, is modified and altered ; and, to return to our original
argument, the ideal of man and woman is certainly
subject to many important transformations.

The ambition of women seems to have been to
establish a standard of their own excellence, essentially different from that which men prized. Their
beauty is more delicate, their manners are more
refined, than any man ever painted ; especially
have they delighted in the internal woman, that
mystery which man has rarely fathomed. They

have developed feelings he could only divine, and
analyzed, with minuteness and power, that change-
able though faithful world which lies enclosed in a
woman's heart. Their success has often been
dearly bought; their men have been exposed to
the reverses which marked the attempts of men
with women. It may be that the sexes know
little of each other, and that little but by contrast;
that man can only see woman's gentleness, and
woman man's strength, and that the more delicate
workings of either must ever escape the other's
penetration and power.

But setting aside this vexed question, and to return to the women of women, we think that,
among the infinite varieties of heroines to which
feminine literature has given birth in England,
Mrs. Smith's may claim to be the earliest and most
successful in personations of the lady—not the elegant, well-bred, fashionable lady, but the lady of
delicate feelings, accomplished mind, and good
manners—the lady who will make a country gentleman's wife. Emmeline and Ethelinda are far
beyond anything similar in contemporary literature, French or English. They have been imitated until their successors have grown common-

place and tame, but the charm of the original models is still such as can be felt.   Strength or depth
of feeling or character we must not ask from
them, the time is not come yet for either quality to
display itself in the heroine; but they are not mere
figures of flesh and blood—they are women amiable
and accomplished, somewhat sad and pensive—the
daughters of a gentle and meditative race, whom
the sorrows of life affect indeed, but for whom the
charms of intellect are ever in store.

In "Evelina" and "Cecilia" it is the world that lies
before the heroines, with its changing, lively scenes;
we see it but little, and under its gloomiest colours,
in all that Mrs. Charlotte Smith, herself a woman
of many sorrows, wrote.   But if too much bitterness tinges her account of a society which Miss
Burney represented with such comfortable powers
of sarcasm, she had a tenderness which the authoress
of "Evelina" never reached.   There is great beauty
and pathos in many parts of "Emmeline;" and
especially affecting is the passage in which Emmeline's uncle—not unkind at heart, not unjust
by will, but rendered harsh and exacting by prosperity—takes up from her table the portrait which
he supposes to be his son's, and feels his anger

melt away on beholding the well-remembered features of his long-lost brother, looking at him with
sad eyes, that seem to reproach him for such severity
to his unprotected orphan child.

"Ethelinda" shows far more power than "Emmeline." The characters are better drawn, the scenes
more vivid, than in Mrs. Smith's first novel,
but the tale is not so pleasing. Ethelinda is the
poor cousin of Lady Newenden, and accompanies
her and Sir Edward Newenden on a visit to their
ancestral mansion near Grasmere. Ethelinda has,
like Emmeline, a tender and pensive turn. She
likes poetry, she likes, too, the lovely lake scenery.
There is great freshness in the short glimpses
which we get of the mountain region; no set
scenes, no set descriptions are these, but clear,
vivid pictures, that make the evening star rise once
more above the mountain's ruddy peak, that make
us feel the coolness of the rippling lake, and bring
the pleasant sound of the mountain waterfalls.
In one of those romantic excursions Ethelinda met
with a young man, Montgomery by name, who, on
a second occasion, saves her from drowning in the
waters of the lake. She becomes known to his
widowed mother, a woman of refined mind, and

a passion—rapid, romantic, and true—begins.   It
is well-nigh hopeless, for Ethelinda's father is poor,
her brother is a spendthrift, and Montgomery has
nothing.   Whilst the lovers look on this gloomy
future as patiently as they can, Sir Edward Newenden, Ethelinda's host, is still more unhappy.   His
wife's ill-temper and caprices have alienated his
affections, and he has, unfortunately, bestowed
them on Ethelinda.   From first to last this gentleman's character is very finely drawn ; his passion
is guilty, but it is founded on all that can excuse it.
Ethelinda's beauty and virtues, her tenderness to
his children, neglected by their unnatural mother,
have conquered his feelings, but not his principles.
He is mortal enough to be jealous of Montgomery,
to be reluctant to see him become Ethelinda's
husband, but he is too noble to use unworthy acts to estrange the lovers, or prevent Ethelinda's happiness.   Of that there seems
little prospect.   Her brother's extravagance causes
him to be imprisoned for debt, and her father dies
of a broken heart.   Montgomery and Sir Edward
Newenden do all that friendship and love can do to
avert these calamities, but uselessly.   Their own
lot is not a happier one than Ethelinda's ; her lover

goes to India, to seek his fortune there and amass
wealth; his wife's misconduct adds new bitterness
to Sir Edward Newenden's hopeless love. Had
he chosen Ethelinda, or one like her, instead of the
vain and heartless Maria Maltravers, how different
his fate would have been!

Her father's death, by rendering Ethelinda a
dependent, gives her the experience of a
variety of homes. For some time her lot is cast
with two ladies of very opposite temper, and who
both may claim to be characters: Miss Clarinthia
Ludfort, her cousin, who dresses like the Shep-
herdess of the Alps, in Marmontel's tale, a tender,
sensitive, selfish creature, is one; the other is Miss
Newenden, who talks, feels, and acts like a sports-
man, loves nothing but horses, and keeps a
hunting lodge. From these two uncongenial companions the delicate and refined Ethelinda gladly
escapes to the society of Mrs. Montgomery, in the
vale of Grasmere. Prosperity and sorrow alternately visit that retreat. Mrs. Montgomery
recovers a long-lost and wealthy brother, whose
kindness places her beyond want, and it is on a
visit to the generous Harcourt that Ethelinda
learns the wreck of Montgomery's ship.

The circumstances which precede the discovery read like the dawn of Mrs. Radcliffe's school. Lord Hawkhurst's seat lies near that of Mr. Harcourt, and in that nobleman's mansion his brother, who was also Ethelinda's father, was born. The young girl visits it almost as a stranger—uncared for, unheeded by her relatives. She wanders to a deserted room, quiet and ancient, in which her eyes are struck by a portrait of her father, painted in his youth. Gazing through the open window, she can see her father's grave in the still, green little churchyard below. The aspect of life, the knowledge of death, unite to move her heart; daylight is fading away from the silent room and the quiet landscape, murmurs arise in the old mansion, the wind sweeps along the corridors, terrors which she cannot define affect the orphan girl—she tries to fly, and faints. The next morning this presentiment of coming evil is explained. Montgomery is dead—or, rather, he is thought to be dead. And so skilfully is the generous and amiable Sir Edward Newenden portrayed, that when his wife's flight and death make him a free man, and allow him to confess his affection for Ethelinda, we almost regret her fidelity to her first lover.

The scene in which, overheard by Montgomery, she finally rejects Sir Edward Newenden, recalls, and probably suggested, that in which Morton hears Lord Evandale press his suit to Edith Bellenden. The termination, however, is not so tragic. Sir Edward Newenden allows the lovers to be happy, and departs, not to return until absence and reason have cured him of his passion. Ambition has no room in Montgomery's heart, and his days are happily spent with Ethelinda in the vale and by the romantic lake of Grasmere.

The heroine is subordinate in " The Old Manor House," Mrs. Smith's finest imaginative effort, but it has other merits. It is her best and most interesting novel, though, like all she wrote, it is tinged with despondency and sadness. In vain does she make heroes and heroines happy in the end : the spirit of disappointment ever broods over the tale.

No better introduction to the "Old Manor House" can be found than the opening pages of this well-told story :—

" In an old manor house in one of the most southern counties of England resided, some few years since, the last of a family that had for a long series of years possessed it. Mrs. Rayland was

the only survivor of the three co-heiresses of Sir
Hildebrand Rayland, one of the first of those to
whom the title of baronet had been granted by
James the First. The name had been before of
great antiquity in the county, and the last baronet
having only daughters to share his extensive pos-
sessions, these ladies had been educated with such
very high ideas of their own importance that
they could never be prevailed upon to lessen it, by
sharing it with any of those numerous suitors who,
for the first forty or fifty years of their lives, surrounded them ; and Mrs. Barbara, the eldest, and
Mrs. Catherine, the youngest, died single—one at
the age of seventy, and the other at that of sixty-
eight—by which events the second Mrs. Grace
saw herself, at the advanced age of sixty-nine, sole
inheritor of the fortunes of her house, without any
near relation, or, indeed, any relation at all, whom
she chose to consider as entitled to possess it after
her death."

Relations, however, Mrs. Grace Rayland has—
the Somerives, in whose veins flows " a portion of
that blood which had circulated in those of the
august personage Sir Orlando de Rayland," but
they are descended from a degenerate Miss Ray-

land, who married a yeoman; and Mrs. Grace
Rayland does not know how far it is just to herself, to them, and to society in general, to acknowledge the relationship.

The character of this haughty, selfish, jealous
woman is excellently sustained throughout. She
lives away from the freedom of modern manners,
in a solemn world of her own, and everyone who
enters that charmed circle must adopt her ante-
diluvian notions. She keeps within her ancestral
pride as within an impregnable fortress. Capricious, mistrustful, and supercilious, she main-
tains the Somerives in a slow fever of suspense.
What will become of her vast property when she
is gone to her venerable ancestors? No one
knows, not even the reader. Orlando, Mr. Somerive's handsome younger son, seems to have a
chance, but who can answer for the fancies of
Mrs. Grace Rayland. This admirably drawn
character, wholly free from caricature or exaggeration, seems to have been suggested to Mrs. Charlotte Smith by that of Queen Elizabeth. She tells
us herself that—

" Though, like another Elizabeth, she could not
bear openly to acknowledge her successor, she was

as little proof as the royal ancient virgin against
the attractions of an amiable and handsome young
man, whom she loved to consider as the child of
her bounty, and the creature of her smiles."

This very amount of favour is, like Elizabeth's,
perilous to its object.   The least indiscretion,
especially of the kind that points to love, may ruin
Orlando for ever.   Mrs. Lennard, the sour housekeeper, has a niece on whom she has bestowed the
romantic name of Monimia.   What Orlando's
feelings are towards this young girl accident discovers to her aunt, and nearly betrays to Mrs.
Rayland herself.

"Mrs. Rayland had been long confined by a fit
of the gout; and the warm weather of Whitsun-
tide had only just enabled her to walk, leaning
on a crutch on one side and on Mrs. Lennard on
the other, in a long gallery which reached the
whole length of the south wing, and which was
hung with a great number of family pictures. Mrs.
Rayland had peculiar satisfaction in relating the
history of the heroes and dames of her family,
who were represented by these portraits. Sir Roger
de Coverley never went over the account of his
ancestors with more correctness or more delight.

Indeed, the reflections of Mrs. Rayland were unin-
terrupted by any of those little blemishes in the
history of her progenitors that a little bewildered
the good knight; for she boasted that not one of the
Rayland family had ever stooped to degrade himself
by trade, and that the marriage of Mrs. Somerive,
her aunt, was the only instance in which a daughter
of the Raylands had stooped to an inferior alliance.
The little withered figure, bent down with age and
infirmity, and the last of a race which she was
thus arrogantly boasting—a race which, in a few
years, perhaps a few months, might be no more
remembered—was a ridiculous instance of human
folly and human vanity, at which Lennard had
sense enough to smile internally, while she affected
to listen with interest to stories which she had heard
repeated for near forty years. It was in the midst of
her attention to an anecdote which generally closed
the relation, of a speech made by Queen Anne to the
last Lady Rayland on her having no son, that a
sudden and violent bounce towards the middle of
the gallery occasioned an interruption of the story,
and equal amazement in the lady and her confi-
dante; who, both turning round, not very nimbly,
indeed, demanded of Monimia, who had been sit-

ting in one of the old fashioned bow-windows, of which the casement was opened, what was the matter ? "

Monimia knows, but will not tell; for Orlando is the offender, and she is the cause of the offence. As he passed through the court to go to cricket in the park, he saw her sitting at the window, and threw up his ball to startle her, instead of which it flew into the room and irreverently struck the picture of Sir Hildebrand himself ; "who, in armour, and on a white horse, whose flanks were overshadowed by his stupendous wig, pranced over the great gilt chimney-piece, just as he appeared at the head of a county association, in 1707." Mrs. Lennard has some suspicion of the truth, but wards off the danger by laying the blame on the wainscot and odd noises of the gallery, " which, if one was superstitious, might sometimes make one uneasy. Many of the neighbours, some years ago, used to say to me that they wondered I was not afraid of crossing it of a night by myself, when you, ma'am, used to sleep in the worked bedchamber, and I lay over the housekeeper's room. But I used to say that you had such an understanding, that I should offend you by showing any

foolish fears ; and that all the noble family that
owned this house, time out of mind, were such
honourable persons that none of them could be supposed likely to walk after their decease, as the
spirits of wicked persons are said to do. But, however, they used to answer, in reply to that, that
some of your ancestors, ma'am, had hid great sums
of money and valuable jewels in this house, to save
it from the wicked rebels in the time of the blessed
martyrs ; and that it was to reveal these treasures
that the appearances of spirits had been seen, and
strange noises heard about the house."

This judicious appeal to Mrs. Rayland's prejudices and pride is successful with that lady, but
Mrs. Lennard privately questions her niece, learns
the truth, and rewards her candour with a box on
the ear, and a stern and imperative injunction to
hold no sort of intercourse with Orlando. Youth
is obstinate, and its promises are worth little;
what can no longer be done openly is done in private; and though Monimia is only fourteen, though
Orlando is little more than a boy, the dawn of
future love appears.

Orlando is the agreeable young hero who so long
held an honourable place in fiction. He is hand-

some, generous, brave, daring, and ardent. Monimia is more ignorant than Emmeline or Ethelinda,
but she has their gentle tenderness. Her weakness
is one which they shared, and to which the heroines
of women are still liable : she is too sensitive, too
easily frightened, and she weeps too much and too
often. The number of times she is near fainting
during her stolen interviews with Orlando is irritating, and the facility with which her tears flow
is childish. The heroines of men, with all their
softness, have stronger nerves than the heroines of
women ; for man likes a woman to be gentle
and yielding, but he does not like her to weep—
the sight of her tears is painful when it is not
provoking.

But though she is somewhat puerile and ignorant, Monimia is pretty and engaging. She be-
lieves in ghosts, and, believing in them, is naturally
afraid of them   Orlando is anxious to eradicate
superstition from the mind of his mistress ; he is
also desirous of improving her education ; he persuades her, since they cannot meet by day, to come
to his sitting-room in the middle of the night, and
study there with him till morning. The ancient
chapel of the manor, and staircases and passages

enough to frighten more courageous girls than Monimia, put her fortitude to a severe proof. With an imprudent disregard of her reputation, which his youth alone excuses, Orlando insists on these interviews that nearly frighten her out of her senses, but they are marked by a delicate feature which only a woman could have conceived in that coarse age: neither her lover nor Monimia talk of love. The holy innocence of childhood, the passionless love of early youth, keep these meetings pure in word as well as deed.

Whilst Orlando is making love, the troubles and cares of the Somerive family increase. Philip, his elder brother, is a gambler, a spendthrift, and a profligate; Isabella, his handsome sister, agrees to marry old General Tracy, and elopes with his nephew; to crown all, Orlando receives a commission, and goes off to fight the American rebels. Mrs. Rayland parts kindly from him, but gives him no positive assurance of her future intentions. Indeed, we should not soon come to an end were we to specify all the delicate traits with which her character is evolved, without the aid of dramatic action—always a difficult matter. The perplexity in which her haughty reserve keeps Orlando's father is admirably shown. What is to be done with Orlando, now of man's estate? A friend suggests business; but suppose Mrs. Rayland should take offence at this low ambition. She is consulted, her reply is a masterpiece of diplomacy.

"Mrs. Rayland, having called for her writing materials, which seldom saw the sun, and being placed in form at her rosewood writing-box, lined with green velvet, and mounted in silver, produced, at the end of four hours, the following letter, piquing herself on spelling as her father spelt, and disdaining those idle novelties by which a few superfluous letters are saved :—

"Raylande Hall, 12th day of September, A.D. 1776.

"SIR, MY KINSMAN,—I have received youre letter, and am oblidged by youre taking the troubbel to informe me of youre family affaires. In respecte to your daughter, Philippa, must begge to be excused from givving my opinion, not haveing the pleasure to knowe the gentlemen, and being, from my retired life, no judge of the personnes charractere, who are remote, and in bisness, as I understande this personne is ; wherefore I can onelye there upon saie, that doubtless you, being,

as you are, a goode and carefulle father, will take
due care and precaution that youre daughtere shall
not, by her marriage, be exposed to the mischances
of becoming reduced by bankruptcies, and other
accidents, whereby peopel in trade are oft-times
grate sufferers. But your care herein for youre
daughter's securitye is not to be questionned.
Furthermore, respecting youre youngest sonne,
Mr. Orlando, he is very certainelye at youre dis-
posal also, and you are, it may be, the most com-
petent judge of that which is fitting to bee done
for his future goode and advantage. I wish him
very well; he seeming to me to be a sober, promising, and well-conditioned youthe; and such a
one as, were I his neerer relation, I shoulde
thinke a pitye to put to a trade. I am at present
alwaies glad of his companie at the Hall, and
willinge to give anye littel encourragement to his
deseir of learninge in the liberal sciences, fitting
for a gentleman, the wich his entring on a shoppe
or warehouse would distroye, and put an ende to.
However that maye bee, I saie again that you,
being his father, are to be sure the propperest
personne to determine for him, and he is dutie-
fullie inclined, and willinge to obey you. Yet, by

the discourse I have had with him thereuponne, it doth not appear that the youthe himself is inclined to become a dealer, as you purpose.

"Heartilie recommending you in my prayers to the Disposer of all goode giftes, and hoping He will directe you in all thinges for the well-doing of your family, I remaine, sir, my kinsman, youre well-wisher and humbel servant,

"GRACE RAYLANDE."

With this cautious letter, which may mean nothing or anything, the Somerives must needs be content. In many words, Mrs. Grace Rayland has told them what they knew, that the father of a family is the best judge of his own concerns. Mr. Somerive detects, however, a glimmering dislike for trade in this epistle; the rich woman's reluctantly implied preference decides Orlando's fate—he enters the army.

No less characteristic and consistent is her conduct when Orlando accepts the challenge sent by Sir John Belgrave, whom he has found trespassing on the sacred precincts of the Rayland demesnes, and insulting the defenceless Monimia, His father is in agony at the thought that his best

and most dearly loved son should peril his life in a
duel. Mrs. Grace Rayland, on the contrary, is
struck with the spirit her favourite displays in de-
fending her injured right. Whilst the anxious
father places his hopes on her interposition, the
ancient lady exults at the idea of seeing the de-
stroyer of her pheasants, and the invader of her
demesnes chastised, and is even surprised and
offended at Mr. Somerive's uneasiness. What is
a duel in comparison with the honour of the
Raylands and the integrity of their territory?
She even hints, in her displeasure, that this
parental timidity is the effect of that admixture of
plebeian blood from the alloy of which Orlando
alone seems free.

The duel does not take place, for Sir John
Belgrave withdraws his challenge; and though
Mrs. Rayland has grace enough not to be disappointed that her favourite runs no risk, no tender
rejoicing at his escape marks the favourable issue
of this affair of honour. Her lurking resentment
takes a placable shape enough. Her neighbours,
the Stocktons and the Belgraves, are upstarts—
they make a great show, but they can be conquered
on their own ground. General Tracy has, with

singular condescension in a man of family, eaten
their dinners, but why should not Mrs. Rayland
show him what she can do without the help of
"kickshaws and French frippery, spoiling whole-
some dishes ?"

"If I had my health," cried Mrs. Rayland, as if
animated anew with a truly British spirit—"if I
had my health, I would ask the favour of General
Tracy to dine at Rayland Hall.   Indeed, I would
request his company to the tenant's feast at my
own table, and show him, if he is too young a
man to remember it, what an old English table
was when we were too wise to run after foreign
gewgaws, and were content with the best of everything, dressed in the English fashion by English
people."

The tenant dinner does take place, and gives
Mrs. Charlotte Smith an excellent opportunity of
indulging her satirical humour at the expense of
the Hollybourns, a clerical family.

Mrs. Hollybourn, a lady of precise and formidable demeanour, sits next to Mrs. Rayland;
opposite her sits the doctor himself, " a dignified
clergyman, of profound erudition, very severe
morals, and very formal manners; who was the

most orthodox of men, never spoke but in sen-
tences equally learned and indisputable, and held
almost all the rest of the world in as low estima-
tion as he considered highly his own family, and,
above all, himself."

The only child of this accomplished pair is
worth some consideration; she acts no important
part in the story, though her parents kindly
destine her for Orlando, but it is curious to contrast Miss Ann—Jane—Eliza Hollybourn, " who,
equally resembling her father and her mother, was
the pride and delight of both," with the accomplished model young lady of to-day.

" Possessing something of each of their personal perfections, she was considered by her
parents a model of loveliness; and her mind was
adorned with all that money could purchase. The
wainscot complexion of her mamma was set off
by the yellow eyebrows and hair of the doctor.
His little pug nose, divested of its mulberry hues,
which on the countenance of his daughter was
pronounced to be *le petit nez retroussé*, united with
the thin lips, drawn up to make a little mouth,
which were peculiar to his 'better half,' as he
facetiously called his wife. The worthy arch-

deacon's short legs detracted less from the height
of his amiable daughter, as she had the long waist
of her mother, fine sugar-loaf shoulders that were
pronounced to be *extremely genteel,* and a head
which looked as if the back of it had by some
accident been flattened, since it formed a perpen-
dicular line with her back. To dignify with
mental acquirements this epitome of human loveliness, all that education could do had been
lavished ; masters for drawing, painting, music,
French, and dancing had been assembled around
her as soon as she could speak ; she learned Latin
from her father at a very early period, and could
read any easy sentence in Greek ; was learned in
astronomy, knew something of the mathematics,
and, in relief of these more abstruse studies, read
Italian and Spanish. Having never heard anything but her own praises, she really believed herself a miracle of knowledge and accomplishments ;
and it must be owned that an audience less partial
than those before whom she generally performed
might have allowed that she performed very long
concertos, and solos without end, with infinite
correctness and much execution. Then she made
most inveterate likenesses of many of her acquaint-

ances, and painted landscapes where very green
trees were reflected in very blue water. Her
French was most grammatically correct, though
the accent was somewhat defective ; and she knew
all manner of history—could tell the dates of the
most execrable actions of the most execrable of
human beings—and never had occasion to consult,
so happy was her memory, Truster's chronology.
As it was believed, so it was asserted by the doctor
and his wife that their daughter was the most
accomplished woman of her age and country, and
by most of their acquaintance it was taken for
granted."

   This amiable lady Orlando has an opportunity
of rejecting, to Mrs. Rayland's satisfaction.   In
vain Doctor Hollybourn assures her that this
island does not produce a finer couple than her
kinsman and his daughter ; in vain he enumerates
the advantages of this union with unctuous and
pious self-gratulation :—

   " Twenty thousand pounds down, and—I will
say nothing of future expectations—I am, I bless
the Father of all Mercies, in a prosperous fortune.
I have seventeen hundred a-year in Church pre-
ferment ; my own property, which I have realized

in land, is somewhat above twelve hundred. When I have given my girl her little marriage portion, I have still something handsome in the three per cents., and in India stock a trifle more. My brother-in-law, the bishop, has no children, and my daughter will inherit the greatest part of his fortune."

But though Mrs. Rayland loves money, it is her own she likes, not Doctor Hollybourn's. She has other views for Orlando, and in the politics of Rayland Hall it is decreed, with his wish, that he shall be a soldier. 1776 is the date Mrs. Charlotte Smith chose for her story, and her reflections on the American war show sufficiently to what party she belonged. The great struggle was still recent when she wrote, and the Church, the aristocracy, the slave-trade, and the American war evidently engaged much of her attention. It was the age of revolt against all the old powers, and Mrs. Smith was on the side of rebellion. After a series of calamitous adventures, Orlando, who has been wounded, a prisoner with the Indians and the French, returns penniless to his native country. He makes his way to the old manor house, and there is much power, descriptive and

pathetic, in the account of his return. Mrs.
Grace Rayland is dead; the estate has gone to
Doctor Hollybourn, and Monimia at first seems
lost. She is recovered, and becomes Orlando's
wife, but the pressure of poverty weighs on the
young pair and on the whole Somerive family.
We have those prison scenes again, without which
—so deeply had she felt the reality—Mrs. Smith
seemed unable to complete a story.

Much of the interest of the tale vanishes, however, with Mrs. Grace Rayland. Orlando's struggles
against poverty, his meeting with his mother, his
discovery of Monimia, his private marriage with
this dearly-loved mistress, and Mrs. Lennard's
remorse, heightened by her second husband's ill-
usage, give interest enough to the close of the
story, but it is not pleasing interest. Thanks to
the tardy penitence of Monimia's aunt, the real
will of Mrs. Grace Rayland in favour of Orlando
is discovered; the reverend Hollybourn has to re-
fund. Orlando Somerive, now Orlando Rayland,
Bart., becomes the happy owner of the old manor
house.

The great merit of this tale, as of all Mrs.
Charlotte Smith wrote, lies in its truth. Mrs.

Grace Rayland is one of the most finely drawn
characters in the English fiction of the eighteenth
century, and, we will venture to add, to Sir
Walter Scott's praise, "old Mrs. Rayland is
without a rival," that none, save Mrs. Smith,
could have portrayed her. Miss Burney would
have exaggerated, and Mrs. Inchbald would have
satirized her. That truth, which gives Mrs.
Charlotte Smith a Cowper-like fidelity of description in natural objects, also saved her from the
worst of all unreal delineations—that which deals
with human beings. As a general rule, her personages are all living and real; she was liable but
to one mistake, and into this she was led by her own
embittered temper—her heartless people are too
open in their heartlessness. They have not enough
of the decent hypocrisy of life and society, and lay
themselves out with too much complaisance to our
contempt and abhorrence. We feel that when
they say or do anything selfish or ill-natured it is
to waken our detestation. Akin to this mistake
is that of incidents too harassing and painful.
There is a grandeur in tragic sorrows, a holiness
in death ; but the mere anxieties of daily life are
wearisome and small, and must enter sparingly into

the elements of fiction. They narrow the bounds
of that wonderful world, and the reality they
possess is not that great reality on which the
novelist can build safely—that broad truth which
comes home to every heart.

In another attribute of the novelist, description,
Mrs. Charlotte Smith is more at home. She was
one of the first to wield that wonderful power, unknown to the humourists, and to their successor,
Miss Burney. In her that power was very great.
Whatever she painted, a room, a house, a landscape, became visible to the eye. And hers was
not, like Mrs. Radcliffe's, an ideal and romantic
nature, it was the nature we all know, with her
woods, her waters, her skies, and her mute appeals
to the wayward heart. There is great beauty and
tenderness in Orlando's feelings as he wanders,
for what may be the last time, in the demesnes of
the old manor house.

"Just as he arrived at the water, from the deep
gloom of the tall firs through which he passed, the
moon appeared behind the opposite coppices, and
threw her long line of trembling radiance on the
water. It was a cold but clear evening, and,
though early in November, the trees were not yet

entirely stripped of their discoloured leaves; a low
wind sounded hollow through the firs and stone-
pines over his head, and then faintly sighed among
the reeds that crowded into the water; no other
sound was heard, but, at distant intervals, the cry
of the wild fowl concealed among them, or the
dull murmur of the current, which was now low.
. . . . Nature appeared to pause, and to ask
the turbulent and troubled heart of man whether
his silly pursuits were worth the toil he undertook
for them? Peace and tranquillity seemed here to
have retired to a transient abode; and Orlando, as
slowly he traversed the narrow path, over ground
made hollow by the roots of these old trees, stepped
as lightly as if he feared to disturb them."

His heart is subdued and sad, for he is going to
part from Monimia, and he is haunted with visions
of rural felicity. He sees the same spot again in
spring—he is going to meet Monimia—and how
altered was its aspect.

"It was a lovely glowing evening, towards the
end of April. The sun was set, but his beams
still tinged with vivid colours the western clouds,
and their reflection gave the waters of the lake that
warm and roseate hue which painting cannot reach.

The tender green of spring formed to this a lovely
contrast; and where the wood of ancient pines
ceased, his path lay through a coppice of low
underwood and young self-planted firs — the
ground under them thickly strewn with prim-
roses and the earliest wild-flowers of the year.
Hope and pleasure seemed to breathe around
him."

Living visions haunt the scene. "Monimia,"
infinitely more lovely, and, if possible, more
beloved than ever, was the principal figure. He
saw her the adored mistress of that house,
where she had been brought up in indigence,
in obscurity, almost in servitude; this gem, which
he alone had found, was set where nature certainly intended it to have been placed—it was to
him not only its discovery but its lustre was
owing—he saw it sparkle with genuine beauty,
and illuminate his future days, and he repressed
every thought which seemed to intimate the uncertainty of all he thus fondly anticipated, and
even of life itself."

This association between our secret feeling and
the eternal, immutable nature which surrounds us,
is one of the aspects of modern fiction, but it was

long the attribute of poetry; and it was only towards the close of the eighteenth century that it
passed into prose in the writings of Rousseau and
Bernardin de Saint Pierre in France, and of Mrs.
Charlotte Smith and Mrs. Radcliffe in England.
Mrs. Smith, no doubt, felt the tendency of her
age, and yielded to it; but her power is too genuine
for its originality to be doubted—freshness, vigour,
and truth still mark her efforts, and have left their
stamp on all she wrote. A few faults, great faults,
though her cotemporaries thought them slight,
have contributed to make her be too soon forgotten. First of all, Mrs. Smith was not genial: few
women are; just as few women have the true
comic power. The very keenness of their per-
ceptions seem to make them reach ridicule at
once, and too surely, for that good-humour without which there is no comic power, to remain and
co-exist. The same subtlety makes women too
sensitive; they suffer because they are too quick
to detect sorrow and to feel it. That sensitiveness
embittered Mrs. Smith's temper—we miss a gentle,
lenient, and kindly spirit in her writings. She
could not forget her sufferings and her wrongs;
rebellion was rife in her, and revolt, though it may

give momentary power, secures no lasting fame.
Calmness is the attribute of fine minds and of
great natures. They feel deeply, as they see far,
but the serenity of strength, and the steadiness of
conscious power, are ever with them. Miss Burney,
Mrs. Inchbald, Mrs. Radcliffe especially, had
their share of that high intellectual attribute.
Mrs. Smith had not. Fitful, impatient, and
wearied, she sought for relief in composition; and
though she was too superior a woman not to write
much that was excellent, not to produce entertaining books, full of genuine matter and interest, she
failed in what she had talent enough to accom-
plish—in producing a good story. There is something like personal animosity in her delineation of
her hateful characters, and this is a fault, and a
great one; there is decidedly bad temper, a sin that
can rarely be forgiven. Truth, her great charm,
her gift and her power, is thus not without frequent alloy. She is not all true—who is?—and
there is no vivid imagination, no sparkling wit, no
gaiety of mind or heart, no commanding style, to
atone for the inevitable coldness, not to say bitterness, which is the tone of her writings. They remain amongst the most remarkable but least read

productions of the time to which she belonged, stamped with the melancholy fiat—above medio-crity, but below genius.

CHAPTER IX.

MRS. RADCLIFFE.

THERE is a strange tide in the destinies of novels. Imagination and reality seem ever at variance, and each has its hour of triumph. When one prevails the other retires, but as invariably to return as the retreating sea to spread once more along the shore it had forsaken. Romantic stories and tales, that profess to deal with the truths of life, rarely flourish side by side. The regularity with which they sink and rise in public favour is one of the most curious features in the history of fiction. It would seem as if each generation of novel readers, and they are short generations, were bound to slight the labours of its predecessors and

walk in other paths—paths which its successor will
not follow. If the fathers cry, let us worship romance, the lofty, the ideal, their children rarely
fail to exclaim, " Let us have reality ! "— and
wearied of reality, with its aspect bitter and un-
poetic, made such by injudicious admirers, the
third generation, longing for the imaginary and
the improbable, goes back to the wildest tales of
old romance.

The coarse, vigorous novels of Smollett and
Fielding, the minute, exact, and prolix histories of
Richardson, were still high in public esteem, and
Goldsmith's exquisite tale of the " Vicar of Wake-
field " was on its way to fame, when the " Castle
of Otranto, a Gothic Story," appeared. The old
world of chivalry, the wild old visions of other
ages, were called up out of the past. It was a spell,
although the magician was not an adept in his art.
Even in our own day we have seen what fruit this
strange tree bore.

" Shall I confess to you what was the origin of
this romance ? " wrote the author to a friend. " I
waked one morning in the beginning of June from a
dream, of which all I could recover was that I had
thought myself in an ancient castle (a very natural

dream for a head filled, like mine, with Gothic story), and that on the uppermost banister of a great staircase I saw a gigantic hand in armour. In the evening I sat down and began to write, without knowing in the least what I intended to say or relate. The work grew on my hands, and I grew fond of it—add, that I was glad to think of anything rather than politics. In short, I was so engrossed with my tale, which I completed in less than two months, that one evening I wrote from the time I had drunk my tea, about six o'clock, till half an hour after one in the morning, when my hands and fingers were so weary that I could not hold the pen to finish the sentence, but left Matilda and Isabella talking in the middle of a paragraph."

To this dream of a gigantic hand we owe the "Castle of Otranto," the gloomy parent of a gloomy progeny. The tale published in 1764 as a translation, by William Marshall, from the Italian of Onuphrio Muralto, was discovered to be the production of Horace Walpole's elegant and facile pen. In the preface to a second edition the author informed the public that the "Castle of Otranto" was an attempt to blend the two kinds of romance,

the ancient and the modern; and, expatiating on
this theme, he laid bare his mode of action, explaining, at some length, his plan of reconciling
imagination with reality, and of making his
gigantic casque, hand, and foot figure in something like an every-day world, where tyrant
fathers, amorous youths, damsels gently jealous,
and foolish, babbling servants were to act human
parts.

The "Castle of Otranto" was a violent and
painful story, but it was well told, and its union
of the marvellous and the real produced some
curious results — chiefly apparent in English
literature. Thirteen years after the publication of
Walpole's tale appeared "The Champion of
Virtue, a Gothic Story," which in a subsequent
edition changed its title to that of "The Old
English Baron," under which it is now known.

The authoress, Clara Reeve, was in her fifty-
second year when she produced this work, the
only popular one of all that she wrote. Little is
known of this lady, save that she was born in 1725,
and died in 1803, in her native town of Ipswich.
"This story," she said, in her preface to "The
Champion of Virtue," "is the literary offspring of

MRS. RADCLIFFE.   239

the 'Castle of Otranto,' written upon the same
plan, with a design to unite the most attactive and
interesting circumstances of the ancient romance
and modern novel. At the same time it assumes
a character and manner of its own, that differs
from both ; it is distinguished by the appellation of
a Gothic story, being a picture of Gothic times
and manners."

Notwithstanding this assumption, the " Old
English Baron " is a very cold and commonplace
production. The marvellous it deals in has neither
poetry nor imagination. The ghost comes and
goes, and does not thrill us with a strange horror.
We read, and do not feel amazed that the laws of
nature have been violated, that the grave has given
up its dead. The hero's composure is in keeping.
He is set to watch in the haunted rooms, but, his
conscience being pure, he knows no fear—as if the
terror which besets the invisible world were a
matter of conscience.

This story, however, has remained a favourite
with the young, perhaps on account of its boyish
hero, Edmond. It had great, but not uncontested,
success at the time of its appearance. There
always will be a class of minds to whom the super-

natural will be antipathetic and ridiculous. Col-
man's Will declared that—

> " A novel now is nothing more
> Than an old castle and a creaking door,
> A distant hovel,
> Clanking of chains—a gallery—a light—
> Old armour—and a phantom all in white—
> And there's a novel !"

And touching on another weak point of these
tales, but one that belongs more to their chivalrous
character than to their supernatural feature, Will's
friend, Dick, scornfully exclaimed—

> " Draw but a Ghost, a Fiend, *of low degree*,
> And all the bubble's broken."

It was, indeed, inevitable that, in dealing with
ages where birth was everything, authors should
unconsciously forsake the humble, the poor, and
the oppressed classes, to tell us of the fortunes of
the strong and the mighty. But they did so,
without reaching the truth they aimed at. Clara
Reeve designed her " Old English Baron " as " a
picture of Gothic times and manners." She
failed; but probably died unconscious of her
failure, a misfortune which she shared with the
greatest who have made the attempt. In reality,

it is impossible to succeed in painting the Middle
Ages with anything like truth. Clara Reeve, like
Walpole, who preceded, like Sir Walter Scott
himself who followed her, could only give us a one-
sided picture.

The method she followed, which Walpole had
opened, which every one has adopted since then,
is the only one that is feasible, but it is bad. She
gave us the romantic customs of that wonderful
period, customs in which ferocity was so strongly
blended with romance—the lists, the judgment of
God, the law of the sword—things remote from
our own manners; but neither she nor her successors ever dared to give us the rudeness, and with it
the breadth and geniality of those wonderful times.
It could not be. Modern delicacy and refinement
would have shrunk aghast from some of the pictures in the romances that were sung and told
in feudal homes, in the ear of noble ladies, and
with the sanction of grave men.

Thus these pseudo Middle Age tales, from the
"Castle of Otranto" and the "Old English Baron,"
downwards, have all tended to give us the falsest impressions. We have been told of great cruelty, and
we have not felt that it was the inevitable result of

great coarseness. Our ancestors have been shown
to us with singular capacities for bloodshed, because we could bear this, our humanity not having
progressed in proportion with our delicacy ; but of
their joyousness, of that mad mirth which went
hand in hand with deeds heroic or terrible, of that
roughness which pervaded every rank of society,
we have not been told. The knight has been
clothed in modern gentleness, politeness, and refinement, and in that smoothing down of features
offensive to modern taste, the largeness, that great
characteristic of the Middle Ages, and perhaps the
greatest, the manly and noble frankness, have
been irremediably lost.

From this evil Miss Reeve's successor in the
regions of terror, Mrs. Radcliffe, kept clear. She
left historical events and the Middle Ages to the
past, threw the date of her stories only so far back
as to give them a romantic interest, and, far from
imitating any who had preceded her, she became,
by the thoroughly original method she adopted,
the foundress of a new school, not a good one, it may
be, but one so fertile in interest and beauty, spite
its faults, that more than two generations have not
yet exhausted its abundant stores.

In the year 1789 was published a romance—
" The Castles of Athlin and Dunbayne." On
the title-page appeared the till then unknown name
of Anne Radcliffe. The following year she gave
the world " The Sicilian Romance ; " in 1791 appeared " The Romance of the Forest," and " The
Mysteries of Udolpho " in 1794. " The Italian,"
in 1797, closed this series of fictions, which had
won their author great fame and some money. In
1809 she was reported to be dead, and as she did
not contradict the report, her name was duly chro-
nicled in biographical dictionaries, with the usual
amount of praise and blame awarded to her literary productions.

In reality, Mrs. Radcliffe did not die till 1823.
She had begun writing at twenty-five, and she
wrote assiduously for eight years; then she stopped.
It is not likely that she had exhausted her imaginative
store, or that her power was ebbing at thirty-three ;
but fame she had enough of, and she wisely forbore to wait its decline. Money she no longer
needed, and ambition of any kind she had never
known. She quietly withdrew from the scene on
which she had never cared to shine, and survived
her last triumph twenty-six silent, and, spite some

suffering, happy years. These few facts tell us her temper—we may add, her whole life, singular in literary history. The reports of her death she never took the trouble of contradicting; she allowed herself to be reckoned as one that had ceased to be, nay, more, when it was asserted that her diseased mind had preyed on itself, and that, the victim of her own wild imaginings, she had become the inmate of a lunatic asylum, she remained calmly silent. What the world said or thought of her, so long as it affected not her integrity, was a matter of little moment to her in her happy retirement.

An existence so serene and so modest leaves little to biography. The care with which she shunned attention has concealed even the few incidents of Mrs. Radcliffe's life. We know what books she wrote, what journeys she took, and there ends our knowledge. How it fared with her in that inner world which it is both the art and the charm of biography to unravel, we may vaguely surmise, but can never know.

Anne Ward was born in London, in July, 1764. Her parents, William and Anne Ward, were tradespeople, but they could boast some gentle blood. One of the De Witts, in Holland, came to England under the reign of Charles I. He was to reclaim the Lincolnshire fens, with the sanction of Government. The fens were not reclaimed; there was other work going on then; a throne was pulled down and a commonwealth proclaimed. But Mr. De Witt remained in England, near Hull, and from his daughter Amelia, whom he had brought with him an infant, Mrs. Radcliffe's father was descended. Other relatives she had— all wealthier and higher than her own parents— amongst the rest, a Mr. Bentley—of the firm of Wedgewood and Bentley—whom she often visited at Chelsea and Turnham Green. There she met Mrs. Piozzi, Mrs. Montague, Mrs. Ord, and Athenian Stuart.

Anne Ward's education was plain and somewhat formal. She was shy; she showed no extraordinary genius, and the times were not propitious to the development of female intellect. The young girl's person was probably more admired than her mind. She was short, but exquisitely proportioned; she had a lovely complexion, fine eyes and eyebrows, and a beautiful mouth. She had a sweet voice, too, and sang with feeling and taste.

At the age of twenty-three, Anne Ward became
the wife of William Radcliffe, a graduate of Ox-
ford. They were married at Bath, where her
parents resided, but soon removed to the neigh-
bourhood of London. The lover and husband
proved more clear-sighted than relatives or friends.
He appears to have felt and seen that the shy little
lady whom he had married, and the exact little
housekeeper who kept her accounts so accurately,
had more than a fair face and a sweet voice, and
was capable of something beyond writing down
her household expenses. He urged her to write,
her diffidence yielded to his encouragement ; she
made the attempt.

Mrs. Radcliffe's mode of life was propitious to
her first efforts, and calculated to influence the
bent of her mind. Her husband was proprietor of
the *English Chronicle* ; he shared largely in the
management of the paper; he was often out the
whole evening, and did not return till a late hour.
Mrs. Radcliffe thus remained alone with her household tasks and cares both over, and nothing better
to do than to sit down and write a story. On these
long, solitary evenings, spent in a quiet room by a
blazing fire, she wrote those strange tales of hers,

where nothing is real, not even the terror. Sitting
thus alone she imagined that veiled picture which
has thrilled more than one generation, that grandly
conceived Schedoni, the prototype of the modern
villain—Byron's included—and which, in its unnatural wickedness, is as yet unsurpassed. Then
passed before her view the fair face of Emily,
an angel vision in that den of crime, Udolpho;
then Julia fled through the subterranean passage;
then Adeline lingered in the dewy glades of the
forest, or Elena was borne away to that melancholy
house by the sea, where treason and murder lie in
wait for their victim. The task was entrancing,
and bound her by a spell as deep as any she ever
cast over her readers. But she only felt the imaginative charm; the fear she imparted to others
she herself never knew. She wrote rapidly, however; her subject led her on, and time passed unheeded. When her husband came home late she
surprised him by the quantity of manuscript she
had produced in his absence, and it is no discredit
to Mr. Radcliffe's fortitude to add that some of her
chapters were more than he ventured to read alone
in the silence of night. The effect these powerful tales produced on the public mind was pro-

digious.   We must not judge them, now that
the taste in which they were written is exhausted
and palled, by our modern feelings.   The best test
of their worth is contemporary opinion, and tales
which delighted Burke, Fox, and Sheridan, must,
when compared with the novels then published, have
possessed a singular amount of merit.   Publishers
were as generous as the public was admiring; her
two last works, " The Mysteries of Udolpho" and
" The Italian," brought her in, one 500*l.*, the other
800*l.*   But, when the death of relatives placed her
and her husband in easy circumstances, Mrs. Radcliffe ceased to write.   They had no children, none
of the motives or tastes that urge people to seek the
world or mingle in society, and both in the same
feeling retired from the active pursuits of life to a
pleasant independence.

Travelling became their great delight; the
Continent they only visited once, and then they
saw but a small portion of it—Holland and the
Rhine.   Mrs. Radcliffe never beheld the countries
she described so often and so well: France, Italy,
and Switzerland.   But with all the beautiful spots
in her own land she was familiar; and her journals
shew with how keen a love of nature she lin-

gered over their beauty. Books, music, and nature
yielded her their exquisite pleasures, and her life
was spent in the enjoyment of all that intellect,
refined tastes, and leisure can afford of happiness.
Ill-health was the only great drawback to this
pleasant existence. Mrs. Radcliffe was afflicted
with spasmodic asthma during the last twelve
years of her life; and on the 7th of February,
1823, she was carried off, in the fifty-ninth year
of her age, after a few weeks' illness : inflammation of the brain following on inflammation of the
lungs proved fatal to her. Her death was tranquil
and unconscious, for she expired in sleep, between
two and three in the morning. Her remains were
laid in a vault of the chapel of ease, at Bayswater,
belonging to St. George's, Hanover Square, and
with this record ends her history.

Mrs. Radcliffe never moved in literary society.
We have no letters of hers—her journals, though
copious, do not deal with her life, nor even with
her feelings, unless as they were manifested with
regard to scenery. When she took up her pen it
was not to trace any records of herself, but to note
the changing aspects of nature—that great passion
of her life; thus few writers of equal celebrity and

date so modern are less known than she is. She
appears to have been shy, a little formal, reserved
in manner, and too proud to enter any circle where
her full equality was not acknowledged. With
these peculiarities blended a serene philosophy,
rare amongst those who write, and which bespeaks
a fine mind. She who could allow herself to be
proclaimed dead or insane and not remonstrate,
was no ordinary woman. Yet to these general
inventions were added particulars. The Duke of
Rutland's seat, Haddon House, which Mrs.
Radcliffe never saw, was mentioned, in a
tour through England, by a lady, as the very
spot where she had acquired her taste for ancient
and romantic edifices; and Derbyshire, which she
only visited for a few days, was designated as the
place of her confinement through insanity. Her
madness, and the death that was supposed to have
closed it, were also deplored by a clergyman, in an
Ode to Terror, composed in 1810. Through all
Mrs. Radcliffe remained, if not quite unmoved, at
least externally passive. We think that this quiet
endurance, joined to her calm retirement from the
active pursuits of literature at an age when she
might well hope for new successes, though it is

probable that the changing taste of the public would have denied them to her, prove that her life was adorned with that lovely moral strength which, spite the terrors she indulged in, gave her works such remarkable sweetness.

Of these works we will now speak at some length, for they are getting less known daily. The generation that read them in youth is passing away, and unless they are speedily reprinted we must look to remote provinces and old-fashioned libraries for those once celebrated romances. From the great literary centre they have all but utterly vanished.

The truth is, that it is not easy to appreciate the great merit of these well nigh forgotten productions; they require the rarest of all things—rare, at least, in general readers—an exact knowledge of what preceded and what followed them. Mrs. Radcliffe's romances, and those of her imitators, fill up the great gap in imaginative literature which lies between Miss Reeve's "English Baron," itself the offspring of "The Castle of Otranto," and Sir Walter Scott's novels. Miss Burney, Charlotte Smith, Miss Edgeworth, and Mrs. Inchbald belong to a very different school :

the social and domestic. This retrospect alone can make us understand Mrs. Radcliffe's great originality. She did what none had attempted before, and she did it infinitely better than anyone who followed in her track. Great though her faults are, in terror and description she is still unequalled.

CHAPTER X.

THE SICILIAN ROMANCE.—THE ROMANCE OF THE FOREST.

THERE are disadvantages which natural powers, though great, rarely conquer, and one of the greatest is an imperfect education. That of women was neglected, as a general rule, when Mrs. Radcliffe was young, and even when she wrote. There were well-bred ladies who knew not how to spell, and to write decent English was not always one of the accomplishments of the fair sex. Their knowledge, such as it was, rarely went far or deep —opinion, prejudice, and society restricted it within the narrowest bounds, and, as a rule, women lacked that culture from within, without which even genius can achieve no perfect work.

There are in Mrs. Radcliffe's writings passages of great beauty, told in beautiful language, but these productions, one and all, betray a mind which had long lain dormant, and that wakened too late to the consciousness of great gifts. In this she reminds us of her cotemporary, Mrs. Inchbald; but the beauty and the actress, though in many respects far more deficient than Mrs. Radcliffe, had a clear, practical knowledge of life which stood her in stead of much. The authoress of "The Italian" and of "The Mysteries of Udolpho" had only Nature, which she loved tenderly and painted with extraordinary power, and Terror, which she knew wonderfully how to waken. There lay her strength, and it was great.

In character, in penetration, in historical knowledge, in all the minutiæ that prove reading, skill, and a cultivated taste, she failed. She was never vulgar, because her nature was delicate and refined, but she was awkward and ignorant. It was, indeed, one of her misfortunes that, intending to write, she had not the patience to delay her intention and prepare herself for a task which want of knowledge alone could make her find easy. She gained as she progressed, but she also acquired a

manner and became confirmed in faults, and
when perfect knowledge came, imagination had
poured out her stores, and, though not exhausted,
could yield nothing new.

In "The Castles of Athlin and Dunbayne,"
short and imperfect though it is, we find the germ
of her faults and merits as a writer. The characters are mere names. The interest of the
story rests on the most improbable incidents; but
there is a feeling for nature, a power of imagery,
and a command on attention, which betray the
genius of one who, had her judgment and taste
been early cultivated, would certainly have been a
great writer. Had Anne Radcliffe been John
Radcliffe, and received the vigorous and polished
education which makes the man and the gentleman, we might have a few novels less, but we
would assuredly have some fine pages more in that
language where, spite their merit, her works will
leave no individual trace. As one from whom
much has been borrowed, and who left her stamp
on many great minds, Mrs. Radcliffe will ever
remain eminent.

In her first work, "The Castles of Athlin and
Dunbayne," she attempted to tell a Highland

story; she did so with indifferent success. But
our ancestors were not practical or matter-of-fact;
they did not require accurate descriptions of real
places, still less a correct knowledge of national
manners, of costume, or even of history. We are
not told the date of this tale, though it relates to
clan revenge, and to passions the manifestation of
which is matter of record.

Were we not informed that its scene is laid "on
the north-east coast of Scotland, in the most romantic part of the Highlands," we might fairly conclude its characters and incidents to belong to the
wide world of phantasy. The fierce passions of
the middle ages, and the manners of the modern
drawing-room, appear side by side in strange and
incongruous contrast. Young ladies draw and
sketch in castles where there are vaults and dungeons enough to chill the boldest heart, and in the
midst of combats, sieges, and surprises sufficient to
drive away all such lady-like fancies. The flight
of Alleyn, the long-lost heir of Dunbayne, from
his ancestral but inhospitable abode, is fertile in
the images and incidents which thus early took
possession of Mrs. Radcliffe's mind. Malcolm's
castle impresses us as a huge building, full of trap-

doors and gloomy vaults—the vision of a distem-
pered dream. Needless horrors are thrust upon
us. Alleyn, groping his way in the dark, stum-
bles on broken armour, and clasps a dead man's
hand. Why is this incident introduced? To produce a momentary shock; as soon as the object
is accomplished, it is dismissed without further
thought.

In this story, too, we find the germ of what was
to be one of Mrs. Radcliffe's excellencies—fine and
striking simile. Alleyn escapes, but his friend,
Osbert, remains in Dunbayne. A beautiful girl
and her mother, captives like himself, tell him the
story of their wrongs; his first knight-like impulse
on hearing them is to avenge them on their oppressor. He forgets that he is himself in that
oppressor's power, and that his very life hangs on
Malcolm's breath. He quickly returns to reality,
to truth, and to his humiliating powerlessness, and,
as the author finely tells us, "he found himself as
a traveller on enchanted ground, when the wand of
the magician suddenly dissolves the airy scene,
and leaves him environed with the horrors of solitude and of darkness."

The "Sicilian Romance," which appeared in

1790, a year after the "Castles of Athlin and Dunbayne," was justly considered a great improvement on Mrs. Radcliffe's first story. She had now discovered the bent of her mind, and she made no sparing use of the fertile region of romance which once for all she boldly entered. Her descriptive power, too, though it had not yet reached its full meridian, was far more apparent in this romance than in the first, and to the exercise of this power, no less than to the superstitious fear she knew so well how to waken, Mrs. Radcliffe was indebted for a great portion of her success. She exaggerated it, indeed, and not being a quality of the loftiest order, it could not well bear such exaggeration ; but it enabled her to reveal to many minds a taste, a passion, that had lain all but dormant till she came, and which she shared with them. She only wrote as she felt, it is true, but as she felt, few of those who had sat down to write a story had felt before her. For in what novels and romances, till she took up a pen, shall we find places and scenery substituted for the human interest?

The taste for landscape is, like landscape painting, comparatively modern. Antiquity has transmitted to us the fame of her great painters, of her Zeuxis and Apelles, but we know that tragic, lofty histories were all they condescended to paint; landscape was with them what it was with the poets of their age—a background. The few relics of ancient art which we possess do not tend to remove that impression. The inferiority, the subjection of landscape is everywhere apparent.

Landscape is still a background in mediæval pictures; then it grows into the representation of places—it becomes the classical landscape of Poussin or Lorraine—the real landscape of Rubens, and it comes down to us as we know it—an ideal mage of some spot the painter dreamed of, or a more or less exact representation of actual places.

But important though landscape painting has become, it has not reached equality with the representation of man. It is a matter of almost total indifference to children and the ignorant, even to those whose lives are spent in the daily communion of nature; for it is with painting as it is with reality—the refined, the cultivated, the fastidious, who see her least, seem to love and know her best.

In fiction, too, landscape long remained a background. We have seen it, in the novels of Mademoiselle de Scudéry, subordinate and exact—an inventory of nature. It took a far more graceful form in the elegant pages of the Archbishop of Cambray. But the landscape of Telemachus, though sweet, is still a set landscape; streams running through flowery plains, woods full of shade and freshness, grottoes carpeted with moss and clothed with vine or trailing ivy, are its chief elements. Beautiful gardens seem to have been the favourite landscapes of our ancestors, who lived so much more in the country than their landscape loving descendants choose to do. The garden was to them the epitome of nature's delights.

The change which has taken place in this respect is one of the most remarkable features of modern literature. It began with poetry; from fine descriptive fragments, poets indulged in whole poems of description, and from poetry the descriptive passion came down to prose; but there, whether its exponents had not the gift in its full force, or whether the time had not yet come, description paused, and still remained the background for the human story.

Mountain scenery in Rousseau, unless haunted

by passion, and the wildness of heath and mist in Macpherson, unless ghostly shapes drifted in the clouds above, would not do alone. A descriptive poem would find readers; had a critic been asked the question, he would have answered that a descriptive novel would find none.

But though readers had willed it so, though what had been granted to landscape in painting, its right to a separate existence, had not been recognized or asserted in writing, though the public cared more to learn how the quarrel between the lovers ended, than to know how the sun set beyond the blue mountain ridge, there were minds, an increasing multitude, whom landscapes haunted to a sort of pain, while human passions and sorrows left them almost unmoved and cold.

Such a mind was Mrs. Radcliffe's. She wrote landscapes, and she wrote them well, though ideally. The contrast, in this respect, between the descriptions in her novels and the descriptions in her journals is curious and instructive. She was graphic, minute, and exact when she wrote for herself, and she sketched in a few lines what in a book she would have amplified into poetic grandeur. Nothing, for instance, is more unlike her descriptions of antique abodes than this brief view of Rochester Castle: "Solemn appearance of the castle, with its square ghastly walls and their hollow eyes, rising over a bank of the Medway, grey, and massive, and floorless—nothing remaining but the shell."

The picture is complete and impressive, but it lacks that vagueness which must have been a system with her, and which is certainly more suggestive than precision. We may read Mrs. Radcliffe through and through, and we shall never find her noting for her reader, as she noted for herself, the "larks singing among the corn near the shore," or that "surprising appearance of the sea" which she beheld from the summit of a hill on her way to Eastbourne, when it "seemed to rise so high that it could scarce be distinguished from clouds; ships looked like birds in the sky."

These are the details of truth, the poetry of matter of fact, and in her fictions she appealed essentially to the imagination. She did not paint the nature we behold daily, though she knew it in all its changes, but that we dream of in languid, summer mood. Hence her wonderful hold over memory, for, if details charm as we read, it is general impressions we remember.

Her best descriptions, with the acccessory figures, remind us of such paintings as the old masters delighted in. You see lovely valleys, hazy mountains, clear sheets of water, sun-lit castles and noble trees; they are true, but not real; they belong to that unknown world of the mind which is to our daily thoughts what fairyland was formerly to earth. The contemplation of these splendid images is delightful, but if you refer to the catalogue or the guide-book you learn that you have been looking at a flight into Egypt, or at an Herminia in the forest, and that the specks of colour you had disregarded are the sacred or romantic personages referred to. Such are her landscapes, and such, too, her characters, good or evil—mere lay figures. She probably felt it herself, and supplied the deficiency with images more lively than scenery, howsoever grand or melancholy—images of terror; but whatever she wrote, whether she described an ideal Sicily, Venice rising from the sea, or tormented us with gloomy halls and the horrors of a veiled picture, Mrs. Radcliffe painted.

The opening of "The Sicilian Romance" is in itself a picture. It was in this work that Mrs. Radcliffe's power of calling up images first displayed itself

with that dim gorgeousness which ever after characterised her. There is an antique charm about
the introduction. We see the ruins of the castle
of Mazzini before we read the fate of its posses-
sors, as gathered from the old manuscript; we see,
with Julia Mazzini, that figure bearing a lamp,
"proceeding from an obscure door belonging
to the tenth tower, and stealing along the
outside of the castle walls." The sudden death
of the old Steward, his broken confession of some
dreadful crime, seem both connected with this mysterious appearance. Other incidents interfere—
festivity, love—but our inflamed curiosity will not
sleep; the secret irritation is there, and leaves us
no more.

On the return of the stern Marquis of Mazzini
to his castle, his second wife takes possession of the
rooms which had been allotted to his daughters
and their governess, Madame de Menou. They
retire to another apartment, spacious but gloomy,
and uninhabited for years, and forming part of the
southern buildings. They are soon disturbed by
the sound of closing doors, heard in the deserted
rooms below at dead of night. Their brother, Ferdinand, undertakes to watch with them. This part

of the story is interesting and dramatic. Mrs.
Radcliffe calls up the world of old castles and
haunted rooms, and, without crowding terrors on
us, makes a most judicious use of those she chooses
to employ.

" They paused a few moments in the chamber, in
fearful silence, but no sound disturbed the stillness
of night. Ferdinand applied a knife to the door,
and in a short time separated the lock. The door
yielded, and disclosed a large and gloomy gallery.
He took a light. Emilia and Julia, fearful of
remaining in the chamber, resolved to accompany
him, and each seizing an arm of Madame, they
followed in silence. The gallery was in many
parts falling to decay, the ceiling was broke, and
the window-shutters shattered, which, together
with the dampness of the walls, gave the place
an air of wild desolation.

" They passed lightly on, for their steps ran in
whispering echoes through the gallery, and often
did Julia cast a fearful glance around.

" The gallery terminated in a large old staircase,
which led to a hall below; on the left appeared
several doors, which seemed to lead to separate
apartments. While they hesitated which course

to pursue, a light flashed faintly up the staircase, and in a moment after passed away; at the same time was heard the sound of a distant footstep. Ferdinand drew his sword and sprang forward."

Ferdinand discovers nothing, though he nearly loses his life in the ruins. He makes a second attempt, sees a light, and a figure gliding through an arched door; pursues and misses it, and returns baffled to the great old hall, and surveys it with unavailing inquiry.

Here we have Mrs. Radcliffe in all her majestic gloom :—

"It was a spacious and desolate apartment, whose lofty roof rose into arches supported by pillars of black marble. The same substance inlaid the floor, and formed the staircase. The windows were high and gothic. An air of proud sublimity, united with singular wildness, characterised the place, at the extremity of which arose several gothic arches, whose dark shade veiled in obscurity the extent beyond. On the left hand appeared two doors, each of which was fastened; and on the right, the grand entrance from the courts. Ferdinand determined to explore the dark recess which terminated his view, and as he traversed the hall, his imagination, affected by the surrounding scene, often multiplied the echoes of his footsteps into uncertain sounds of strange and fearful import.

" He reached the arches, and discovered beyond a kind of inner hall, of considerable extent, which was closed at the further end by a pair of massy folding doors, heavily ornamented with carving. They were fastened by a lock, and defied his utmost strength.

" As he surveyed the place in silent wonder, a sullen groan arose from beneath the spot where he stood. His blood ran cold at the sound, but silence returning, and continuing unbroken, he attributed his alarm to the illusion of a fancy which terror had impregnated. He made another effort to force the door, when a groan was repeated, more hollow and more dreadful than the first. At this moment all his courage forsook him; he quitted the door, and hastened to the staircase, which he ascended almost breathless with terror."

These passages show us Mrs. Radcliffe in her element, and in all her peculiar power. She suggests terror far more than she seems willing to create it. She shows us a light, a gliding figure,

gloomy halls, and leaves the rest to our imagination. This is her art, and it is a great one. Her
imitators, unable to cope with her in means so
slender, and in effects so sure, accumulated sicken-
ing images to suggest terror, and exhausted their
power before the result was attained. She alone,
skilful and sparing, held imagination subject with
a word, and charmed the minds she thrilled with
the vastness and the sublimity of her pictures.
She terrified, indeed, or, to speak more correctly,
she called up terror, and it came at her bidding;
but even whilst such was her purpose and intent,
she forbore, as a rule, to sicken or appal—a solemn
beauty ever pervaded her gloomiest pages.

Through all these mysteries the tale progresses.
Julia, the heroine, loves the Count de Vereza, and
her father insists on marrying her to a Duke de
Luovo. Her tears, her protests, only cause her to
be locked up ; the wedding-day comes, the bride
has vanished, and is tracked to a convent.
Again she escapes.; but we must not attempt to
analyze this wild story to its happy though tragic
close. Her successive flights—the pursuit of her
betrothed and her father—her escapes, are in the
wildest spirit of romance. We have banditti and

dungeons, scenes of terror and gloom, but told with real poetic power. The shipwreck scene in which Julia and her brother are cast back on the Sicilian shore, is all blackness and horror. We seem to see nothing but dark skies and the sinking ship. The landscape through which the Count de Vereza travels in search of Julia is not a Sicilian landscape, indeed; it is a wild northern land of mountain and heath, but it is a grand landscape, and gives us a feeling of strange depth and vastness. The adventures of the young count with the banditti whom he surprises murdering a traveller, his flight through the intricacies of the ruined monastery, the pursuit of the robbers, and the breathless escape which leads to the vault in which the bodies of murdered travellers were cast, are painted and conceived in the same wild and, spite their horror, imaginative spirit.

It is in character that Mrs. Radcliffe fails; her cruel Abate has no touch of reality. He protects Julia against her father; he threatens him with excommunication, with the sacrilegious revelation of a dying man's confession; and for what?—not to win some fearful prize of ambition or wealth—no, that Julia, a poor, penniless girl, may become a nun.

This is her weakness. When she leaves the supernatural her skill fails. The means she takes for
human ends are as mighty as those ends are small.
It is the heel of Achilles of all she wrote.

Her want of humour is more easily understood.
In his search for Julia the Duke de Luovo meets with
an adventure which Sir Walter Scott transferred to
Ivanhoe. The duke, on knocking at a convent
gate, is informed that the monks are engaged in
prayer, and that he cannot be admitted. He enters
by force, and finds a rosy superior and a company
of friars feasting in the refectory. Who does not
remember Friar Tuck and Richard Cœur de Lion
in Sir Walter Scott's delightful romance? In
Mrs. Radcliffe this is told without spirit, and is
simply indecorous, and not amusing. But the story is
the least successful part of "The Sicilian Romance."
We are led to the end through the most thrilling
adventures, and it closes with a provoking and
tragic explanation of all the perplexing mysteries.

In one of her wild flights Julia takes refuge
in a cavern which leads her to vaults where
she finds her mother, not dead as she was
thought to be, but buried alive by her husband,
whose passion for another woman led him to com-
mit this crime. To the imprisonment of this un-

THE ROMANCE OF THE FOREST.

fortunate lady were owing all the mysterious sights
and sounds which haunted the castle of Mazzini.
Whilst Julia and her mother effect their escape
from this gloomy dungeon, the Marquis discovers
the infidelity of his second wife, who commits sui-
cide after poisoning him. He dies penitent and
acknowledging his crimes, and the tale ends with the
marriage of Julia and her lover, and the peace and
happiness of the whole family in Naples. The castle
of Mazzini, the silent witness of so many heinous
deeds, is left to ruin and solitude.

The very title of the " Romance of the Forest "
is full of promise. It wakens, too, some of the
most delightful associations in English poetry.
Who can forget the wildness and the grace of the
Robin Hood ballads, that opened this lovely line
of forest literature ?—

> " In summer time, when leaves grow green,
>   And birds do sing on every tree."

But it is always summer in those enchanting
woods ; we never hear of frost or snow, or piercing
winds there, as in the bleak plain, or on the desolate moor.

> " For since 'tis fair weather, we'll into Sherwood,
>   Some merry pastime for to see."

Who would not go with the bold outlaw on such
a quest? For as we are told again—

> " When Robin Hood came into merry Sherwood,
> He winded his bugle so clear,
> And twice five-and-twenty good yeomen bold,
> Before Robin Hood did appear."

Another time he is standing in the forest, "all
under the greenwood tree," or, " among the leaves
so gay," when he sees young Allan-a-Dale coming
over the plain, and " chaunting a roundelay.'
But whether he meets the gay young lover,
" clothed in scarlet so red," whether he plunders a
bishop, or conquers the bold curtal friar of Foun-
tain Dale, it is still the merry greenwood with its
sunlit glades; it is still the forest so green, with
its bounding deer, with its wildness and its liberty.

This is one aspect of the forest—one that has
charmed a nation for ages; Shakespeare gave us
another, more lofty, more poetic, and more extensive, in " As You Like It." His Forest of Arden,
in whatever region his delightful fancy may have
placed it, lives for ever, and lives for more than
England. The "melancholy boughs" under which
Orlando found the banished duke; the oak whose
"antique root" peeped out along the brawling

brook, and which heard the soliloquy of melancholy Jacques watching the wounded stag—the shepherd's cot that sheltered sweet, merry Rosalind, have become the world's inheritance.

Yet, spite those lovely images, spite, too, that intuitive love of fresh woodland scenery which is a feature in the English character—a love which has been gradually imparted to Europe, and which shows itself so significantly under the shape and name of the Jardin Anglais—there is a great gap after Shakespeare, and it literally was not until Mrs. Radcliffe published her third romance that the forest appeared once more in its freshness and wild beauty. She had genius enough to do it justice, and she had also that love which is second to genius alone in power. Windsor Forest was one of her favourite haunts, and it is recorded in her life, that in all that noble domain "there was scarcely a tree of importance with the peculiar form of which she was not familiar, and the varieties of whose aspect in light and shade she could not picture in words." No wonder, then, that she gave us the forest with all its dewy freshness, with its sense of wildness, and, what none had done before her, with its mystery. The story

she selected was wonderfully adapted to the impressions she wished to awaken. It is, perhaps,
the least defective of the five she wrote, and
though not the best, it is that which has most
unity of purpose, and which strives least after
that mixture of the real and the supernatural that
was both Mrs. Radcliffe's charm and error.

Our interest is arrested in the first pages, and con-
tinues unbroken almost to the very last. We know
nothing of La Motte and his wife, save that the
husband is guilty and pursued, and that the wife
is unhappy. We see them leaving Paris at midnight; we accompany them in their flight along
the solitary roads, over the wild heath, till they see
the light burning afar, in the lonely house where
the real story opens. His coachman having in the
darkness missed the right road, M. La Motte
alights, and walks to the house on the heath, in
the hope of obtaining information. His inquiries
are answered by wild-looking men, who bid him
enter, then lock him up and vanish. Convinced
that he has fallen into the hands of desperate
thieves, La Motte expects his fate, when his apprehensions are strangely relieved. A beautiful
but weeping girl is dragged in before him by the

same men, a pistol is presented to his breast, and, under penalty of instant death, he is bid to swear that he will at once take the stranger away with him. He may do what he pleases with her, but seen again by her present keepers she must never be. Their threats, and her tears and entreaties prevail; M. La Motte departs with the beautiful stranger, or rather he is taken back with bandaged eyes to his carriage, and the fugitives, now three instead of two, proceed on their ominous journey.

Adeline's story, so far as she can tell it herself, is pregnant with mystery. Her mother died in her infancy; her father, a cold, harsh man, placed her in a convent, where she was brought up with the intimation that she was to become a nun. On her positive refusal to take the vows, her father removed her from the convent, and conveyed her to the wild abode where La Motte had found her, and where she had spent three days in the conviction that her life would be attempted by the sinister-looking men to whose guardianship she had so ominously been left by her unnatural parent. More than this she does not tell, because more she does not know; but we know that there is more behind,

T 2

and around this blue-eyed girl the interest of the
story henceforth centres. Adeline, indeed, is not
a much more interesting heroine than Emily and
Elena in Mrs. Radcliffe's subsequent novels; but
like them, she is a lovely vision enough, and the
background on which she moves is, for some time
at least, thoroughly enchanting.

Not far from Lyons, the travellers find themselves in a vast forest. It is early spring, the
season of all, save autumn, when woods are most
bewitching. The wakening into life of nature after
her long winter slumbers, the tender green of the
young foliage, the wild fragrance of the trees, the
untrodden and grass-grown path below, the tender
gloom above, are all painted by Mrs. Radcliffe
with her peculiar power; but what we especially
feel of this forest is its vastness — it is as wide and
as endless as Fairyland—and when the travellers
come to the ruined abbey, and gaze with awe
on its ivy-clad battlements, we feel a sort of relief
to learn that, wild as this region now looks, man
has been there   The ruin which gives its grace to
solitude also breaks its spell.

"It stood on a kind of rude lawn, overshadowed
by high and spreading trees, which seemed coeval

with the building, and diffused a romantic gloom around. The greater part of the pile appeared to be sinking into ruins, and that which had withstood the ravages of time showed the remaining features of the fabric more awful in decay. The lofty battlements, thickly enwreathed with ivy, were half demolished, and become the residence of birds of prey. Huge fragments of the eastern tower, which was almost demolished, lay scattered amid the high grass that waved slowly to the breeze. ' The thistle shook its lonely head —the moss whistled to the wind.' A Gothic gate, richly ornamented with fretwork, which opened into the main body of the edifice, but which was now obstructed with brushwood, remained entire. Above the vast and magnificent portal of this gate arose a window of the same order, whose pointed arches still exhibited fragments of stained glass, once the pride of monkish devotion."

La Motte enters the abbey, and finds the vast and silent ruin deserted.

" As he walked over the broken pavement, the sound of his steps ran in echoes through the place, and seemed like the mysterious accents of the dead, reproving the sacrilegious mortal who thus dared to disturb their precincts.

" From this chapel he passed into the nave of the great church, of which one window, more perfect than the rest, opened upon a long vista of the forest, through which was seen the rich colouring of evening, melting by imperceptible gradations into the solemn grey of upper air. Dark hills, whose outline appeared distinct upon the vivid glow of the horizon, closed the perspective. Several of the pillars, which had once supported the roof, remained, the proud effigies of sinking greatness, and seemed to nod at every murmur of the blast over the fragments of those that had fallen a little before them."

All this is charming, and, moreover, it is Mrs. Radcliffe's own. Who had described ruined abbeys and forest solitudes before she came and opened that lovely world to fiction? We have had them to satiety since then; ruined abbeys have become commonplace, and Nature's eternal youth alone has saved the forest. But if we could forget all imitations, and read these beautiful pages in their first freshness, how exquisite should we not think them?

An accident to the chaise compels the travellers to spend the night in the ruins, which are not so dilapidated as not to afford them the shelter of substantial rooms.

"The night passed on without disturbance. Adeline slept, but uneasy dreams fleeted before her fancy, and she awoke at an early hour; the recollection of her sorrows arose upon her mind, and yielding to their pressure, her tears flowed silently and fast. That she might indulge them without restraint, she went to a window that looked upon an open part of the forest. All was gloom and silence; she stood for some time viewing the shadowy scene.

"The first tender tints of morning now appeared on the verge of the horizon, stealing upon the darkness—so pure, so fine, so ethereal, it seemed as if heaven was opening to the view. The dark mists were seen to roll off to the west as the tints of light grew stronger, deepening the obscurity of that part of the hemisphere, and involving the features of the country below; meanwhile, in the east the hues became more vivid, darting a trembling lustre far around, till a ruddy glow, which fired all that part of the heavens, announced the rising sun. At first a small line of inconceivable splendour emerged on the horizon, which, quickly expanding, the sun appeared in all his glory, unveiling the whole face of nature, vivifying every colour of the landscape, and sprinkling the dewy earth with glittering light. The low and gentle responses . of the birds, awakened by the morning ray, now broke the silence of the hour, their soft warbling rising by degrees till they swelled the chorus of universal gladness."

Tempted by the security of this solitary refuge, La Motte resolves to fix his abode in it. His wife's remonstrances only strengthen his purpose—here he stays with her and Adeline, and their two servants, Peter and Annette. A few articles of furniture are procured from the neighbouring town; La Motte's fishing and hunting help to provide for the food of his family, and money secures what the forest cannot yield.

A French critic has said, with great truth, that no one knew better than Mrs. Radcliffe how to appeal to the secret superstition innate in the human heart. We think we may add that in making the forest the home of her characters she appealed

to a feeling as subtle, as mysterious, and as deep as
superstition: man's secret though seldom gratified
passion for solitude. It is the passion of childhood
and of youth, of that season of life when the heart
is all ardour and the mind all wealth; when solitude
is not the dreary void it becomes later, but a world
peopled with images lovely and rare, the offspring
of our own thought, and therefore doubly dear.
But solitude is not merely dear to our imaginative
faculties; it is irresistibly alluring to a natural,
though not amiable, feature in every heart—selfishness. It is sweet not to see faces we do not love,
not to hear speech that offends or wearies, not to
feel the cold or searching gaze of the stranger's
eye. It is sweet to fly from all these to the calm
and soothing companionship of our silent mother
nature, and to sink on her bosom to delicious rest.
Some have found it so for days, others for hours;
others, again, unable to break their ties, have never
known the indulgence save in thought or in books.
Delightful to these is " Robinson Crusoe," that bold
struggle of man with nature; and sweet, in its
degree, is the "Romance of the Forest," with its
wild, ruined home, and its mysteries so closely
woven in its wildness.

This is, perhaps, in an artistic point of view, the most remarkable feature in this romance. Adeline's fate, the traditions connected with the Abbey, and which point it out as the scene of some gloomy tragedy, the strange conduct of La Motte, and the incidents of the story, are all blended with a landscape of great sweetness and freshness. The horror never makes us forget the beauty of the forest glades, and their wild loveliness does not attenuate unduly the impressions we receive from what takes place at the Abbey.

The fugitives have not long taken up their abode there before Madame La Motte becomes aware of a strange alteration in her husband. He spends hours in the recesses of the forest, and Peter, his servant, watches him in vain. The terrors of discovery rouse him from his gloom ; a stranger has been inquiring for him. What if it were one of his pursuers ? The Abbey is explored for a hiding place. We enter again subterranean passages and solitary chambers, and again, as ever in Mrs. Radcliffe, all ends in vain alarm. The inquiring stranger who follows La Motte to the Abbey, and surprises Adeline timidly exploring the deserted rooms, whilst the family is concealed in the dark recesses under ground, proves to be M. and Madame La Motte's son Louis, who soon conceives an unreturned passion for his father's young guest.

Adeline's heart, however, is bestowed on a stranger whom she has met in one of the sweetest and wildest recesses of the forest, and who soon appears at the Abbey under romantic circumstances. The family are sitting together on a stormy night, when the noise of a cavalcade outside, and a violent knocking at the gate of the Abbey, fill La Motte with the deepest alarm. Convinced that he is pursued by the agents of the law, he will not admit the strangers, who force an entrance. Madame La Motte screams, Adeline faints, and on coming back to consciousness she sees bending over her the handsome young stranger she had met in the forest. Theodore Peyrou is the companion of an older and more important person, the Marquis of Montalt, proprietor of the Abbey.

Although this gentleman expresses no discourteous intention of sending away his unbidden tenants, his presence exercises a strange impression of fear on La Motte. The Marquis of Montalt becomes a visitor at the Abbey, and persecutes

Adeline with insulting attentions. Louis La
Motte and Theodore Peyrou are gone, La Motte is
gloomy, his wife is estranged—Adeline feels alone
and unprotected.

And now open the terrors of the Abbey—
terrors with which we feel that she is connected.
Strange dreams tell her, in their own solemn language, the tragic history of a young cavalier
whom she follows through galleries and chambers,
and beholds in all the agonies of a violent
death. Her waking visions are no less significant. Urged by the feeling that she is
destined to unravel the secret mysteries of the
Abbey, she steals at night, lamp in hand, along the
solitary corridors, and through the deserted chambers of the ruin. She sees the same rooms, the
same spots which her dream had shown her; she
finds, too, a dagger, eaten with rust, and a manuscript, which she takes away. This she reads in
her room at midnight, with the storm moaning in
the forest, and the wind stirring the worn-out
arras that hides the secret door. Her terrors as
she peruses that scarcely intelligible narrative of a
great crime, written by the ill-fated victim—who
proves to be her own father—are told with great

power, especially when coming to the most dramatic part of the story, and conquered by scenes so terrible, she dare not even raise her eyes, lest, in the glass before her, she should see some strange image near her own.

Farther than this, on the threshold of the supernatural world, Mrs. Radcliffe did not venture. The rest of the story is human enough, though as romantic as any lover of the strange and eventful need wish.

Ignorant of her real parentage, Adeline thinks herself pursued by her father, and seeing that, for some reason or other, La Motte is in the power of the Marquis, and will not protect her against him, she resolves to fly. The attempt only puts her more easily into the power of the Marquis. He has her conveyed to his luxurious villa in the vicinity of the forest, but from this perilous abode she escapes, with the assistance of her lover, Theodore Peyrou. The fugitives are overtaken, however— Theodore wounds the Marquis, who is his colonel as well as his rival; and whilst he is waiting for his trial and condemnation, Adeline is once more removed to the Abbey, now to be kept a close prisoner. Her captivity is short. A seal has

betrayed her real birth to the Marquis, who is her
uncle, and the murderer of her father, his elder
brother. His love turns to aversion and fear; a
crime had rid him of the parent—a crime shall rid
him of the child. Whilst La Motte is expatiating
on her singular loveliness, and endeavouring to
heighten the Marquis's passion, he coldly and
sternly asks for her death. Guilty though he is,
La Motte shrinks from this crime. At the risk of
his life, he saves Adeline by favouring her escape
with Peter, who takes her safely to Savoy—
whilst the enraged Marquis causes La Motte to be
arrested and cast into prison, as having, some months
before, robbed and wounded him in the forest.
This was the secret of his hold on the fugitive,
and it now proves the ruin of both. La Motte is
tried and condemned, but his accusations against
the Marquis, strengthened as they are by other
and weightier testimony, drag down his accuser to
more than his level. One is sentenced to death,
and pardoned; the other does not wait for condemnation, but dies by his own hand.

The story has other complications. Adeline's
escape into Savoy—her kind reception in the
family of the Pastor La Lue, who proves to be

Theodore's father—the fate of Theodore himself, who, after being condemned to death, is pardoned and restored to liberty—the discovery of Adeline's birth, and her accession to rank and wealth—fill up a goodly space in the story. But the scene of that story, far more than the tale itself, is the secret of Mrs. Radcliffe's power; and from the moment of Adeline's final flight from the Abbey, and of La Motte's arrest, the forest is forsaken, and with the forest vanish the wildness and beauty of the romance, in which, as Sir Walter Scott justly says, there are scenes "which could only have been drawn by one to whom nature had given the eye of a painter, with the spirit of a poet."

CHAPTER XI

THE MYSTERIES OF UDOLPHO.—THE ITALIAN.

THE " Romance of the Forest " appeared in 1791, a
year after the " Sicilian Romance." Mrs. Radcliffe, however, took three years to mature her
longest and most popular work, " The Mysteries of
Udolpho," published in 1794. It is difficult to
speak of this remarkable book ; it can be compared
to none save Mrs. Radcliffe's other works, and it
is superior to all in power and conception. The
" Castles of Athlin and Dunbayne " is a weak and
pale story; the " Sicilian Romance " leaves impressions, but no distinct remembrance. "The
Romance of the Forest" is graceful, but easily
forgotten ; but it is impossible to read " The Mysteries of Udolpho," and forget it.

Its faults, as well as its beauties, both wonderful, are stamped with a mighty impress. Bad
taste, bad grammar, characters weakly drawn,
deep terrors that resolve into commonplace incidents, strange and horrible adventures that lead
to nothing, beset us on every side. What of that?
We are led through scenery soft, splendid, and grand,
such as we may have imagined, but have never
seen; through a sublime world, peopled with beings
real enough to arrest attention, sufficiently unreal
not to harrow; beings that seem called forth from
nothing to yield us a sense of freshness and
repose in the very midst of terror, so unlike all we
know are both that terror and they.

The tale opens in France, in the year 1584; but
the date is immaterial; the story belongs to no
time, and Mrs. Radcliffe did not even attempt historic truth. Her characters are modern; they
speak, think, and act like modern people. Their
delicacy and sensitiveness do not suit the savage
scenes and ruthless deeds midst which they are
thrown. An armed knight, rising from his stony
tomb and conversing with a lady in powder patches
and hoops, would not seem a stranger sight than

the banditti who surround the delicate, prudent, and sensible Emily.

The opening of the story is marked by more sweetness than power. The serenity which the author preserved whilst she thrilled her readers is always apparent in the calm pictures she gives us of virtue. The happy family of the St. Auberts is pleasingly painted. We are introduced to them in a calm southern home. The Pyrennees "gleam through the blue tinge of air," the Garonne winds through a happy and fertile land; prosperity, content, delicate and refined pleasures, fill the abode in which Emily, the only surviving child of her parents, has grown up beautiful, happy, and beloved. Madame de St. Aubert dies, and the health of her husband, which had been failing for some time, is further impaired by grief. The physician orders change of scene and milder air, and father and daughter set out on a slow, leisurely journey for Provence.

Pleasure journeys were the events and the romance of Mrs. Radcliffe's life. She liked travelling. She liked that vivid succession of images and pictures; the road left behind, the road spreading on, the strange, dreamy charm of passing

motionless through so much earth and sky   She
had a wonderful eye for scenery, and a wonderful
power in describing it : no wonder that she filled
her tales with journeys.   Her heroes and heroines
seem wanderers upon earth.   Happy or persecuted,
they are ever winging their flight to the charming
regions, or to the grand and sublime scenes Mrs.
Radcliffe so often described and never saw.

The journey of St. Aubert and his daughter is
described and narrated with wonderful minuteness,
with a deep feeling of nature and a close acquaintance with all her beauties.   We are told all the
tints of the landscape, and how those " various
colours melted in distance into one harmonious
hue that seemed to unite earth with heaven ; " the
white foam of the waterfall " seen amid the darkness of the pines," the heathy mountains " along
which the solitary sheep-bell was heard," come
before us with a stroke of the pen.   We wander
through mountains and by the edge of precipices
day after day, ever on the brink of adventures
which do not come, or which come shorn of their
marvels.

The chief incident is that the travellers meet
with a handsome young hunter enjoying the

u 2

romantic name of Valancourt, who quickly falls
in love with Emily, and whose silent passion is
silently returned. After parting from him at
Arles, St. Aubert and his daughter reach a wood
where they wander, vainly seeking shelter. The
tale now darkens, and the mysteries begin. St.
Aubert is ill, all but dying; it is night, and a
gloomy figure, that speaks in hollow tones, besets
the path of the travellers. A white château glim-
mers through towering trees, but superstitious
horror seems to seize all that are questioned concerning this dwelling. A hospitable cottage is
reached, and the wonders continue. Exquisite
music is heard on the moonlit air. It has been
heard years, and no one has ever seen the musician.
Then come dark hints concerning a sad story connected with Château le Blanc. The fate of its
late mistress, the Marchioness of Villefort, is also
alluded to, and the old peasant narrator would
say more, did not St. Aubert agitatedly check
him.

The next day St. Aubert dies, and a mystery
which he will not reveal to his child dies with him.
She returns to her lonely home and obediently
burns, without reading them, the papers hidden in

a recess of his study. A few words that fill her
with horror, and which she cannot help reading,
and the portrait of a beautiful lady, awaken our
curiosity in vain ; no explanation appears. Emily's
sorrows now deepen. After permitting, then for-
bidding, Valancourt's addresses, her aunt, Madame
Chéron, marries Signor Montoni, a sinister Italian,
who suddenly takes his wife and her niece to
Italy.

Once more a journey leads us on through magnificent scenery. Instead of the Pyrennees, we
have now the Alps beset with snows and clouds—
" a world of chaos " which only makes more enchanting to the view the Arcadian landscapes of
Italy that lie smiling below. Piedmont, Lom-
bardy, the Brenta, then Venice herself, are called
up before us with wonderful power.

" Nothing could exceed Emily's admiration, on
her first view of Venice, with its islets, palaces,
and towers rising out of the sea, whose clear surface reflected the tremulous picture in all its
colours. The sun, sinking in the west, tinted the
waves and the lofty mountains of Friuli, which
skirt the northern shores of the Adriatic with a
saffron glow, while on the marble porticoes and

colonnades of St. Mark were thrown the rich lights and shades of evening. As they glided on, the grander features of this city appeared more distinctly; its terraces, crowned with airy yet majestic fabrics, touched, as they now were, with the splendour of the setting sun, appeared as if they had been called up from the ocean by the wand of an enchanter, rather than reared by mortal hands."

Mrs. Radcliffe never saw that splendid and lovely city which she described so vividly. Byron, who saw it, borrowed from her, or rather took the fine image with which the above passage closes. Who does not remember the famous stanza which opens the fourth canto of Childe Harold's Pilgrimage ? —

> " I stood in Venice, on the Bridge of Sighs,
>   A prison and a palace on each hand ;
>   *From out the waves I saw her structures rise,*
>   *As at the stroke of an enchanter's wand.*"

The serene beauty of the evening, the exquisite music that floated on the air, the gliding of the barge on the waters, and " the fairy city that appeared approaching, to welcome the strangers," are all described with vividness and power. Venice appears, in Mrs. Radcliffe's pages, as we all remem-

ber her in our dreams, gay, luxurious, and splendid ;
not the desolate Venice of our own days, decaying
in her lagunes, but a noble queen, whose ships
were on every sea, whose voice was heard in many
a council.

Even the quiet, prudent Emily is charmed with
the fascinations of Venice. The palace of Montoni is, like its master, full of contrasts. The
apartments are furnished with costly magnificence,
or show the most squalid neglect. Montoni gam-
bles, sees very doubtful company, and neglects his
wife, who, however, unites with him to persecute
Emily into marrying Count Morana. Indeed, her
consent not being considered requisite for this
union, it is decided that it shall take place spite
her resistance. Madame Montoni is anxious that
Emily should become a countess—Montoni's motives are more substantial. Count Morana, who is
desperately enamoured, will relinquish all claim to
Emily's little French property, for the sake of
securing her hand, and no maiden's tears and nays
shall make Montoni give up this unique chance of
despoiling his wife's niece.

The bridal day is appointed, the bridal presents
are purchased, when unexpected relief comes to

Emily. Montoni, for having assisted in the escape
from Venice of a murderer named Orsino, one of
his accomplices and friends, is obliged to leave the
city in the dead of night, and finds it expedient to
take refuge in his castle of Udolpho, in the Apennines.

The splendours of Venice, the verdure of the
banks of the Brenta, are now left behind. We
enter the gloomy world of mountain and forest,
roads that climb painfully up the steep rocks, lead
us through unknown regions, on to that dark
castle which may be called the real hero of this
strange tale. The approach to it is wonderfully
well told.

"Towards the close of day, the road wound into
a deep valley. Mountains, whose shaggy steeps
appeared to be inaccessible, almost surrounded it.
To the east, a vista opened, and exhibited the
Apennines in their darkest horrors; and the long
perspective of retiring summits rising over each
other, their ridges clothed with pines, exhibited a
stronger image of grandeur than any Emily had
yet seen. The sun had just sunk below the top of
the mountains she was descending, whose long
shadow stretched athwart the valley, but his slop-

ing rays, shooting through an opening of the cliffs, touched with a yellow gleam the summits of the forest that hung upon the opposite steeps, and streamed in full splendour upon the towers and battlements of a castle that spread its extensive ramparts along the brow of a precipice above. The splendour of these illuminated objects was heightened by the contrasted shade which involved the valley below.

" 'There,' said Montoni, speaking for the first time in several hours, ' is Udolpho.'

" Emily gazed with melancholy awe upon the castle which she understood to be Montoni's ; for though it was now lighted up by the setting sun, the gothic greatness of its features, and its mouldering walls of dark grey stone, rendered it a gloomy and sublime object. As she gazed, the light died away on its walls, leaving a melancholy purple tint, which spread deeper and deeper as the thin vapour crept up the mountain, while the battlements above were still tipped with splendour. From those, too, the rays soon faded, and the whole edifice was invested with the solemn duskiness of evening. Silent, lonely, and sublime, it seemed to stand the sovereign of the scene, and to frown defiance on all who dared to invade its solitary reign."

This is a masterly description. The terror and awe of Udolpho are not lost in minute architectural details; the grand, lonely castle stands before us real, though mysterious, a visible terror. And terrible within is this gloomy abode; the grass-grown courts, the gothic halls, the cold vast chambers, and endless corridors depress us strangely. From the moment that we pass with Emily beneath the raised portcullis, and cross the threshold of the heavy gates, we feel brooding over us a fate like that which hung above the dwelling of the Atridæ. It is the very place for ruthless deeds and horrible legends. The broken tales of the way in which it came into the possession of Montoni are suggestive of treachery and murder. Its late mistress, Signora Laurentini, a beautiful, violent woman, who had rejected Montoni's suit, left the castle one evening to walk in the woods around it, and never returned to it in the flesh, though her spirit was said to be seen on the ramparts. Montoni, as her next heir, took possession of her inheritance, not without strong suspicion of foul play.

His gloomy bearing and stern speech do not

belie the imputation of some hidden crime. Signor
Montoni has dropped the gentleman of Venice; he
now looks more like a captain of banditti taking
refuge in his lair, than like a feudal lord returning to his ancestral home.

And what a home is this! Savage-looking and
armed men prowl about it. They sit at Montoni's
table, and share those gloomy banquets where the
poisoned wine hisses in the pure Venetian glass,
and the faithful goblet is shattered to pieces in
the hands of the host; with Montoni they hear
that sullen voice which taunts him with crime at
his own table; furious passions possess them.
Ate herself seems to have come to Udolpho. With
her fair startled face and her bright locks imprisoned in a net of pearls, Emily glides about
that iniquitous place like a spirit of Heaven that
has mistaken its way and strayed into the home of
the accursed. Our heart sickens for her, for we
hear the clash of drawn swords, the tumult of
desperate men fighting in closed halls, the
moans of the wounded; we see, too, the track of
blood that leads up the steep steps of the turret,
to which her aunt had been conveyed as suspected of the poisoning, and all these things

come upon us one after the other without
confusion, clear, terrible, and distinct, though
seen through a certain mystery which is not
vagueness.

It is difficult, if not impossible, to analyze the
wonderful effect produced by the machinery Mrs.
Radcliffe put in motion; we may think little of
it; we cannot, whilst we read, disregard it, or, to
speak more correctly, we must either disregard
it utterly or feel it in all its force. Its great,
its marvellous power is all the more surprising
that it depends on the skilful introduction of
trifling incidents minutely told; some with a
positiveness and an irritating secrecy that show
consummate art, till we unfortunately come to
the touchstone of explanation. The most remarkable is the well-known incident of the veiled
picture.

In the castle of Udolpho, in one of its lone-
liest chambers, there is a picture veiled with black
silk. No one knows what lies behind that veil;
but it is something terrible. Emily's curiosity is
roused; she resolves to lift the veil and know the
secret. She crosses rooms deserted and desolate,
and reaches the door of the mysterious chamber,

We will tell the rest in the author's own brief words.

"Emily passed on with faltering steps, and having paused a moment at the door, before she attempted to open it, she then hastily entered the chamber and went towards the picture, which appeared to be enclosed in a frame of uncommon size that hung in a dark part of the room. She paused again, and then with a timid hand lifted the veil; but instantly let it fall—perceiving that what it had concealed was no picture, and, before she could leave the chamber, she dropped senseless on the floor."

She nearly faints a second time on recovering consciousness, then she flies to her own room filled with horror and dread. What had she seen? We do not know; we are not told till the end of the book. We do not enter the chamber again, for the door is locked, and no one else sees the picture or raises the black silk veil; but the effect is produced —the circumstance has seized on our imagination, and haunts us with a sort of torment. This was what the author wanted, and truly her object is accomplished.

In such matter lies the true power of this story.

There is no lack of incident, but incident itself is
subordinate to the terror that ever surrounds and
magnifies it like those changing mists that float
across the brow of mountains and increase the
huge forms they seem to veil.

Emily's fate progresses in this evil home. She
is carried away, rescued, sent to Tuscany, and
brought back. Her aunt dies, and she seeks for
her in strange, fearful chambers, with chairs of
torture and memorials of old cruelty. At length
she escapes from Udolpho with the assistance of
her maid Annette, Ludovico, Annette's lover, and
a French prisoner named Du Pont, who entertains
a hopeless passion for Emily, whom he saw and
knew in her native Provence.

The escape is well told, and is sufficiently dramatic ; but Du Pont, already unfortunate in his love,
is unfortunate with the reader. He rudely and
unnecessarily dispels all our most agreeable terrors.
A strange mysterious form on the ramparts sent
the sentinel wild with fear, frightened Annette,
and haunted the dreams of Emily — it was Du
Pont's. Sweet music was heard in the evening—
music mysterious and spirit-like—it was Du Pont's.
The voice of an invisible speaker taunted Montoni

in his own halls, and dared him to proceed in his
iniquitous plans of despoiling the orphan Emily—
it was Du Pont's voice. These discoveries break
the charm of Udolpho. That gloomy, frowning
home of bad men is almost an imposture. It has
laid claim to supernatural terrors which it does not
possess, to crimes of which it is guiltless. And it is
not merely our faith in Udolpho that is shaken;
spite the wonderful art of the writer, we cannot
believe again in the supernatural of Château le
Blanc. We know that it will be all explained and
made clear.

Château le Blanc belongs to the Count of Villefort. It is that haunted deserted abode to which
Emily and her dying father attempted to make
their way in the melancholy wood where they
heard the wonderful music. The château is now
inhabited by the count, his wife, and his son and
daughter. Some charming, indeed lovely, descriptions are given of the surrounding scenery, and especially of those beautiful shores above which rises the
convent of St. Claire, in which St. Aubert is buried.
The vessel bearing Emily, Du Pont, and their at-
tendants is beset by a fearful storm and almost
wrecked in the bay, near the convent. The tra-

vellers disembark, and are hospitably received by
the Count of Villefort and his family.

But Mrs. Radcliffe did not excel in the picture
of manners. The intercourse of Emily with her
new friends leaves us cold ; we do not care even
about the amiable Du Pont, and Valancourt, who
appears once more, and has unfortunately become
something like a profligate, is not more interesting.
Emily, yielding to prudence, breaks with him, and
what is it to us ? The ghostly stories of Dorothée,
the old housekeeper—the likeness of, Emily to the
late Marchioness of Villefort — the sad story of
that lady, who was the original of the miniature
in Emily's possession—are to us matters of much
more moment than Valancourt's fate or Emily's
distress. Some of the most effective passages in
the book are in this latter part of it. The narrative of Dorothée, the visit which she and Emily
pay to the apartment of the late marchioness,
locked up for the last twenty years, the sad aspect
of those lonely chambers with their decaying
relics of the dead lady, between whom and
Emily we feel a mysterious affinity, are all admirably told. The haunted room, too, is impressively
described.

A strange hold do old dwellings and old apartments possess on Mrs. Radcliffe's mind. She
brings them before us with a power that has never
been surpassed. A mixture of distinctness and
gloom hangs around those ancient homes. The
air is heavy, the light is dim, the repose of years
floats around us; we feel the weight of time and
the power of bygone generations. It is a complete abstraction from the present, from daily life
and its turmoil. Vivid and beautiful is the description of an ancient saloon, with its old Venetian mirrors, which, "instead of a blaze of lights,
and a splendid and busy crowd," now only reflect
"the rays of one glimmering lamp." We have
had Mrs. Hemans's mirror in the deserted hall
since then.

> " Now, dim, forsaken mirror,
>   Thou givest but faintly back
>   The quiet stars, and the sailing moon
>   On her solitary track."

And many a moralist in prose and song has given
us lonely chambers, and, with them, images of
life's sad brevity, until we are sated, but Mrs.
Radcliffe's deserted halls are her own truly. First
she saw them in that imaginary world where they

lay forgotten and unknown, and, calling them forth, she gave them " a local habitation and a name."

A band of robbers explains the mysteries of Château le Blanc. The unearthly music is played by an insane nun wandering at night, and that nun, who poisoned the Marchioness of Villefort, St. Aubert's sister, is the Signora Laurentini. Montoni is thus proved innocent, and we are not even allowed the veiled picture; the veil is raised, scarcely to our satisfaction.

" A member of the house of Udolpho, having committed some offence against the prerogative of the Church, had been condemned to the penance of contemplating, during certain hours of the day, a waxen image made to resemble a human body in the state to which it is reduced after death. This penance, serving as a memento of the condition at which he must himself arrive, had been designed to reprove the pride of the Marquis of Udolpho, which had formerly so much exasperated that of the Romish Church; and he had not only superstitiously observed this penance himself, which he had believed was to obtain a pardon for all his sins, but had made it a condition in his will, that his descendants should preserve the image, on pain of forfeiting to the Church a certain part of his domain, that they also might profit by the humiliating moral it conveyed."

Montoni is thus proved to be no murderer. His stern figure thus loses some of its power over the imagination, and his mysterious and tragic end in the dungeons of Venice is too hastily told to impress us. Udolpho, on the death of the Signora Laurentini, goes to a Monsieur Bonnac, a French relative of hers, and, being thus a mere matter of inheritance like any ordinary castle, forfeits all claim to mystery and dignity. The tale ends with the marriages of Emily and Valancourt, and of her newly discovered cousin, Blanche de Villefort, with the young St. Foix.

In her closing words the author tells us what she wishes us to consider the real purport of her story :—

"Oh! useful may it be to have shown that, though the vicious can sometimes pour affliction upon the good, their power is transient and their punishment certain; and that innocence, though oppressed by injustice, shall, supported by patience, finally triumph over misfortune."

x 2

And did Mrs. Radcliffe really write to enforce truths so excellent, but so commonplace? It is hard to believe it. But a certain formality, a love of trite and too evident conclusions, always were her errors. She had a fine, but not a free imagination—she never dared, in her published works at least, to go beyond the most ordinary explanations of the most supernatural-looking incidents. She lured with mighty promises, and never ceased to disappoint with the strangest and most provoking tameness. Her scenery alone was ever noble and complete; her characters were an almost total failure—not that she lacked the power of fashioning them so as to wear the semblance of life, but that the same timidity which compelled her to explain all her wonders away kept her back from what she would have considered too daring an infringement of conventional types. Her heroes and heroines are mere shadows—her characters, good or bad, have scarcely a separate existence—her domestics are of one foolish, talkative, timid, honest progeny.

In this latter respect Mrs. Radcliffe has very evidently acted on the rule laid down by Horace Walpole in his preface to the second edition of "The

Castle of Otranto": "With regard to the deport-
ment of the domestics, on which I have touched in
the former preface, I will beg leave to add a few
words. The simplicity of their behaviour, almost
tending to excite smiles, which at first seem not
consonant with the serious cast of the work, appeared to me not only not improper, but was marked
designedly in that manner. My rule was nature.
However grave, important, or even melancholy
the sensations of princes and heroes may be, they
do not stamp the same affections on their domestics;
at least, the latter do not, or should not be made
to express their passions in the same dignified tone.
In my humble opinion, the contrast between the
sublime of the one and the *naïveté* of the other sets
the pathetic of the former in a stronger light.   The
very impatience which a reader feels while delayed
by the coarse pleasantries of vulgar actors from
arriving at the knowledge of the important catastrophe he expects, perhaps heightens, and certainly
proves that he has been artfully interested in the
depending event."

Walpole appeals to the supreme authority of
Shakespeare as confirming these principles, but Mrs.
Radcliffe did not go so high as this great model,

next to nature for truth, and so often identical
with her; the garrulous, meddling, foolish Bianca
whom Walpole painted, the officious, fearful
chamber-maid who can never come to the point or
say the right thing, was assuredly the parent of her
Annette, of Peter, Ludovico, and the rest of the
tribe.

Her best attempts in character are the extremely
good or the extremely bad; she saw human nature as
she saw everything, larger than truth, magnified into
unnatural virtue or unnatural wickedness. St.
Aubert is perfectly good, tender, amiable, and true;
Schedoni is as entirely bad, perfidious, cruel, and
relentless; but though neither is true, there is
great sweetness in one, and great power in the
other. One is like Mrs. Radcliffe's ideal landscapes,
and the other like her savage, frowning castles.
Both belong to the world of the imagination, and
cannot be tried by the laws of real, every day life.

" The Mysteries of Udolpho" appeared in
1794; Mrs. Radcliffe took three more years to
perfect her last work, " The Italian," which was not
published till 1797. It was not so successful as its
predecessor, but its power, and in some respects its
superiority, were acknowledged. The character of

Schedoni alone, so strongly conceived, so relentlessly developed, proved that timidity, not weakness, was Mrs. Radcliffe's great error. "The Italian" is a better constructed and told story than "The Mysteries of Udolpho," and if its terrors are not so highly wrought, neither is the explanation so disappointing; moreover, it has less of the false supernatural, which is the most injudicious feature in her tales; its horrible is of the dark, savage, genuine kind; for whilst we believe in human depravity we cannot refuse our credence to the profound corruption of a Schedoni, or to the infamous baseness of Spalatro.

In his account of Mrs. Radcliffe and her works, Sir Walter Scott has spoken with praise of the introductory chapter of this story. It is, in its way, one of the most remarkable she ever wrote, and marvellously suggestive.

Some English travellers visiting a Neapolitan church are struck with the singular figure of a man passing through the pillars of the portico with folded arms and downcast looks. Startled by the sound of the visitors' steps, he enters the church and vanishes. His tall, thin figure, somewhat bent, his sallow face, and the fierce look of his eye

impress the strangers; they question a friar concerning him, and learn with surprise and horror
that he is an assassin who has taken sanctuary.
He is seen entering a confessional, concerning
which an Italian, one of the party, volunteers some
strange statements.

" ' Observe yonder confessional,' added the
Italian, ' that beyond the pillars on the left of the
aisle, below a painted window. Have you discovered it ? The colours of the glass throw, instead
of a light, a shade over that part of the church,
which perhaps prevents your distinguishing what
I mean.'

" The Englishman looked whither his friend
pointed, and observed a confessional of oak, or
some very dark wood, adjoining the wall, and re-
marked also that it was the same which the assassin
had just entered; it consisted of three compart-
ments, covered with a blank canopy. In the
central division was the chair of the confessor,
elevated by several steps above the pavement of the
church; and on either hand was a small closet or
box, with steps leading up to a grand partition, at
which the penitent might kneel, and, concealed
from observation, pour into the ear of the confessor

the consciousness of crimes that lay heavy on his heart.

" ' You observe it,' said the Italian.

" ' I do,' replied the Englishman, ' it is the same which the assassin had passed into, and I think it one of the most gloomy spots I ever beheld ; the view of it is enough to strike a criminal with despair.'

" ' We in Italy are not so apt to despair,' replied the Italian, smilingly.

" ' Well, but what of this confessional?' inquired the Englishman. ' The assassin entered it.'

" ' He has no relation with what I am about to mention,' said the Italian, ' but I wish you to mark the place, because some very extraordinary circumstances belong to it.'

" ' What are they?' said the Englishman.

" ' It is now several years since the confession which is connected with them was made at that very confessional,' added the Italian; ' the view of it, and the sight of the assassin, with your surprise at the liberty which is allowed him, led me to a recollection of the story. When you return to the hotel, I will communicate it to you, if you have no pleasanter mode of engaging your time.' "

The story follows; at the close only do we hear again of the confessional, but the effect is produced, and this introduction, which Sir Walter Scott likened to the vaulted gateway of an ancient castle, leads us to a wonderful tale of romance and mystery, with, now and then, that gorgeous and luxuriant scenery in which Mrs. Radcliffe delighted.

"The Italian" begins, like an old Italian novel, with the meeting of the lovers in a church of Naples. Vincenzo di Vivaldi, the only son of noble and wealthy parents, is the lover, Elena Rosalba, a beautiful orphan girl, living discreetly under the guardianship of an aunt, in a villa looking over the bay, is his mistress. Against this love are conjured two formidable opponents: the Marchioness of Vivaldi, and her confessor, Father Schedoni, both dark and vigorously drawn characters. The latter is a graphic portrait.

" His figure was striking, but not so from grace; it was tall, and though extremely thin, his limbs were large and uncouth, and as he stalked along, wrapt in the black garments of his order, there was something terrible in his air, something almost superhuman. His cowl, too, as it threw a shade over the livid paleness of his face, increased its

severe character, and gave an effect to his large
melancholy eye which approached to horror. His
was not the melancholy of a sensible and wounded
heart, but apparently that of a gloomy and fero-
cious disposition. There was something in his
physiognomy extremely singular, and that cannot
easily be defined. It bore the traces of many passions, which seemed to have fixed the features they
no longer animated. An habitual gloom and severity prevailed over the deep lines of his countenance, and his eyes were so piercing that they
seemed to penetrate, at a single glance, into the
hearts of men, and to read their most secret
thoughts; few persons could support their scrutiny,
or even endure to meet them twice. Yet, notwithstanding all this gloom and austerity, some rare
occasions of interest had called forth a character
upon his countenance entirely different; and he
could adapt himself to the tempers and passions of
persons whom he wished to conciliate with astonishing facility, and generally with complete triumph.
This monk, this Schedoni, was the confessor and
secret adviser of the Marchesa di Vivaldi."

Serene and beautiful is the love this dark monk
opposes. Vivaldi's private marriage with Elena is

agreed upon, and, accompanied by Signora Bian-
chi, the two lovers have excursions in the delightful
Bay of Naples. They go " to Puzzuoli, Baiæ, or
the woody cliffs of Pausilippo," midst scenes described with that lovely but ideal colouring which
Mrs. Radcliffe adopted.

" As, on their return, they glided along the
moonlit bay, the melodies of Italian strains
seemed to give enchantment to the scenery of its
shore. At this cool hour, the voices of the vine-
dressers were frequently heard in trio, as they
reposed, after the labour of the day, on some pleasant promontory, under the shade of poplars; or
the brisk music of the dance from fishermen on
the margin of the waves below. The boatmen
rested on their oars while their company listened
to voices modulated by sensibility to finer eloquence
than it is in the power of art alone to display; and
at others, while they observed the airy, natural
grace which distinguishes the dance of the fishermen and peasant girls of Naples. Frequently, as
they glided round a promontory, whose shaggy
masses impended far over the sea, such magic scenes
of beauty were unfolded, adorned by these dancing
groups on the bay beyond, as no pencil could

do justice to. The deep, clear waters reflected
every image of the landscape—the cliffs branching
into wild forms, crowned with groves whose rough
foliage often spread down their steeps in picturesque luxuriance; the ruined villa, on some bold
point, peeping through the trees; peasants' cabins
hanging on the precipices, and the dancing figures
on the strand—all touched with the silvery tint
and soft shadows of moonlight. On the other
hand, the sea, trembling with a long line of radiance, and showing in the clear distance the sails of
vessels stealing in every direction along its surface,
presented a prospect as grand as the landscape was
beautiful."

Beautiful, indeed; but not the Bay of Naples.
Mrs. Radcliffe's Italy is that we imagine, not that
we see. The abduction of Elena, carried away by
masked men, leads us through other scenes. We
pass then through the romantic landscape which
Mrs. Radcliffe may be said to have invented, and
which she painted with a master hand. Another
world, another sky, other scenes than the real are
these.

Vivaldi tracks Elena to the convent where she
has been taken, and helps her to escape; but

agents of the Inquisition arrest the fugitives as a
priest is on the point of marrying them, and
after a desperate contest, in which Vivaldi is
wounded, the lovers are parted once more. Their
fate is in the pitiless hands of the Marchioness
and of Schedoni. These two guilty hearts meet in
evil counsel and agree to sin; the one through
wickedness and malice, the other through passion
and weakness. Working on her incensed pride
with pitiless skill, Schedoni makes the Marchioness
herself condemn the innocent Elena to death.
Their interview in the church of San Nicolo is one
of the most powerful passages in the story.
Schedoni has brought the Marchioness to the end
he aimed at, but he cannot subdue the terrors of a
conscience less hardened than his own.

" ' Avoid violence, if that be possible,' she added,
immediately comprehending him—' but let her
die quickly! The punishment is due to the crime.'

" The Marchesa happened, as she said this, to
cast her eyes upon the inscription over a confessional, where appeared, in black letters, these awful
words, " GOD *hears thee!*" It appeared an awful
warning; her countenance changed; it had struck
upon her heart. Schedoni was too much engaged

by his own thoughts to observe or understand her silence. She soon recovered herself; and considering that this was a common inscription for confessionals, disregarded what she had at first considered as a peculiar admonition; yet some moments elapsed before she could renew the subject.

" ' You were speaking of a place, father,' resumed the Marchesa—' you mentioned a '——

" ' Ay!' muttered the confessor, still musing; 'in a chamber of that house there is '——

" ' What noise is that ?' said the Marchesa, interrupting him.

" They listened. A few low and querulous notes of the organ sounded at a distance, and stopped again."

" ' What mournful music is that ?' said the Marchesa, in a faltering voice; ' it was touched by a fearful hand. Vespers were over long ago.'

" ' Daughter,' said Schedoni, somewhat sternly, ' you said you had a man's courage. Alas! you have a woman's heart.'

" ' Excuse me, father; I know not why I feel this agitation; but I will command it. That chamber ?'

"'In that chamber,' resumed the confessor, 'is a secret door, constructed long ago.'

"'And for what purpose constructed?' asked the fearful Marchesa.

"'Pardon me, daughter; 'tis sufficient that it is there; we will make a good use of it. Through that door—in the night—when she sleeps'——

"'I comprehend you,' said the Marchesa—'I comprehend you. But why—you have your reasons no doubt—but why the necessity of a secret door in a house which you say is so lonely —inhabited by only one person?'

"'A passage leads to the sea,' continued Schedoni, without replying to the question. 'There, on the shore, when darkness covers it; there, plunged amidst the waves, no stain shall hint of'——

"'Hark!' interrupted the Marchesa, starting, 'that note again.'

"The organ sounded faintly from the choir, and paused as before. In the next moment a slow chaunting of voices was heard, mingling with the rising peal, in a strain particularly melancholy and solemn."

" ' Who is dead ?' said the Marchesa, changing countenance; ' it is a requiem!'

" ' Peace be with the departed !' exclaimed Schedoni, and crossed himself ; ' peace rest with his soul!'

" ' Hark to that chaunt,' said the Marchesa, in a trembling voice, ' it is a first requiem ; the soul has but just quitted the body.' "

" They listened in silence. The Marchesa was much affected : her complexion varied at every instant; her breathings were short and interrupted, and she even shed a few tears; but they were those of despair rather than of sorrow."

Unavailing is that tender and solemn warning sent forth by the dead. The Marchesa moved a moment, for she is both weak and violent, soon returns to her original designs, in which Schedoni abets her with the cold badness of his character. Whilst Vivaldi, in the dungeons of the inquisition, is a prey to all the ingenious perfidy of his tormentors, Elena, destined to a fate more terrible, is born away to the melancholy abode of Spalatro on the Adriatic. Never, unless in " Udolpho," has Mrs. Radcliffe invested a human dwelling with more terror than this the true abode of murder and treason.

Every moment that passes is full of the most harassing suspense, every motion of Spalatro's is ominous and boding. Escape there is none. The solitude of that dreary dwelling, the wild sea-shore in front, the savage forest behind, impress us more than the bars of a dungeon. Here human aid is as impossible a boon as human mercy, for none come here with a thought of pity in their hearts. The agony of Elena in this dreary prison is complete, she has no hope, no illusions; she knows why she was brought there, what fate awaits her. Food she will not touch, it is poisoned, sleep she cannot indulge in, lest the murderer should steal on her slumbers, it is a lingering and harrowing death, in which imagination and reality strive for terror; at length relief comes.

Schedoni is to do the deed. A dagger in his hand, he enters her room at night. Worn out with watching, Elena has fallen asleep; he steals to her bedside, and removes the handkerchief that covers her bosom. A portrait is clasped around her neck. The monk sees a man's face, and in that haughty countenance of a dark cavalier he recognizes his own features. A terrible light breaks on his mind. Father Schedoni was once the Count of Bruno, and the sleeping girl is his daughter.

Elena wakens, and finds this strange father with more of fear than of joy. Why was he there? What mean his wild looks and broken words? What brought to her pillow the dagger which she discovers the next morning? Is he her saviour, or did he mean to be her murderer? His behaviour on their journey from Spalatro's house back to Naples, his ready use of the dagger and pistol, his dark looks and long silence, heighten her perplexity. She reaches safely the convent Della Pietà, where her father leaves her, and where, after some time, she discovers her mother in the nun Olivia, who has been transferred to it; but of Vivaldi, though his mother dies suddenly, neither she nor any one knows anything.

Vivaldi is imprisoned, and his accuser, Schedoni, caught in his own toils, soon joins him. Spalatro, his old accomplice, and a monk whom he had used to waylay Vivaldi with mysterious warnings, have turned against him, and revealed the Count of Bruno's crimes. Condemned for the murder of his elder brother, whose widow he had married by force, Schedoni faces his doom with stern resolve. Spalatro is dead, but the monk his betrayer still lives to be avenged on him. Schedoni, by some means which he dies without explaining, takes a poison which the traitor shares. The latter dies first, and Schedoni expires with a fearful yell of triumph and revengeful joy. To the last he sustains his demon-like nature—an unnatural and horrible but powerful conception.

Cold and tame, after such scenes, comes the announcement that Elena is not the daughter of Schedoni, whom ₁the portrait misled, but of his murdered elder brother, and we hear with composure of her marriage with Vidaldi, who, exonerated from the sin of heresy by Schedoni's deathbed confession, is once more a free man.

The success of "The Italian" was great; it was Mrs. Radcliffe's last published work. Perhaps she felt or thought that she could not go beyond this mighty picture of evil, which generated, or at least, certainly influenced the Byronic hero. Some prudential feeling she must have had, for she continued to write. A visit to Kenilworth suggested the story of " Gaston de Blondeville," which was published three years after her death, with "Saint Alban's Abbey," a poem of some length, besides minor pieces.

This posthumous production is a singular combination of the Walter Scott and Radcliffe elements. Conscious, at last, of her ignorance in archæology, and vexed, no doubt, that so easy a source of power should have been closed on her so long, she went into the other extreme, and from a complete disregard of historic truth, she indulged herself with an amount of architecture and costume which sat awkwardly on her story, and injured it. Knowledge came too late, and Mrs. Radcliffe showed her wisdom in not publishing this tardy attempt. She began by being a disciple of Walpole, and from Walpole to Walter Scott the transition was too great. Her first manner was not good, but it was her best.

After an introductory chapter, a visit to Kenilworth Castle, and an enticing account of a certain chest with an old manuscript in it, "Gaston de Blondeville," which purports to be an abridgement of the same manuscript, opens in the following style :

" It was at the feast of Saint Michael that King Henry, the third of his name, with his queen and sundrie nobles of the realm, and a marvellous train of estates and gentils, came to keep court in Ardenn, at his castle of Kenilworth."

And thus it proceeds with a prolix and minute account of the procession, and we are compelled to conclude that Mrs. Radcliffe, when leaving off the faults of her own manner, could only exchange them for the defects of another school.

Attendant on the king's person is a young Provençal knight, Gaston de Blondeville, of doubtful repute, though high in the monarch's favour. A cry of " Justice, most noble Henry!" raised in the crowd by a stranger, who swoons on beholding the king's favourite, gives us the clue to a forcibly told but too tedious tale of wrong.

The stranger, Hugh Woodereeve, a merchant of Bristol, openly accuses Sir Gaston de Blondeville of robbery and murder. His story is to the purport that, three years before, travelling with a very large sum of money in his possession, and being in company with three other travellers, two of them merchants of good repute, and the other a kinsman of his own, they were attacked in the forest of Ardenn, when about two miles from

Kenilworth, and robbed of nearly all they carried. His kinsman, Reginald de Folville, was killed in the contest, and Gaston de Blondeville was the murderer. The accusation, though haughtily repelled, and unsupported by proof, is pertinaciously maintained by the merchant. The King, however, has the accuser imprisoned in the tower, whilst the accused spends his evening merrily with Queen Eleanor and his beautiful betrothed, Lady Barbara.

The rest of the story is a struggle between right and wrong. In this respect it is a far nobler conception than any of Mrs. Radcliffe's previous efforts; for though she always strove to show the might of virtue and truth, she did so in a conventional spirit, with blue-eyed heroines and gallant young heroes. In this work a plain merchant, of middle age, a man oppressed with the cares of life, is compelled by his conscience to become the vindicator of truth, and ends by being all but the martyr of justice. No attempt is made to initiate us into Hugh Woodereeve's inner nature, or to interest us unduly in his favour; yet we are drawn towards him, for we feel that he is no ordinary character. His persistency in the accusation,

which every step he takes renders more fatal to
himself, his resignation, his grief for his dead kinsman, his sorrow for his family, and his unyielding
integrity, make him the fit impersonation of
oppressed truth and righteousness. With this
feeling of justice blend some of Mrs. Radcliffe's
old incidents, told with all her old power.

The midnight visit of the Prior of Saint Mary's,
an accomplice in the murder, to the imprisoned
merchant, is invested with a peculiar sense of fear.
A parley takes place between the monk and the
captive through a grated opening in the cell.
Shall the prisoner withdraw the bolt or not, which
will enable his visitor to enter? On that slight
incident seems to hang Hugh Woodereeve's fate;
and when, after many denials and much hesitation, he admits the Prior—when, yielding to his
arguments, he leaves his prison, and follows him
through the vast and gloomy windings of the
sleeping castle, until a sudden flash of the torch
across that dark face wakens memory, and makes
him exclaim, "I know you!"—expectation, wound
to the highest pitch, can scarcely bear to follow
him in his flight to the sanctuary, where he takes
refuge.

Mrs. Radcliffe was less fortunate in her introduction of the only genuine supernatural agency she ever used. In vain spectral sights, warnings, tokens, and a real ghost meet us at every corner. She who knew so well how to waken those dim and undefined fears which haunt the human heart, knew not how to deal with the realities of the supernatural world. There is ten times more terror in the wild flight of Hugh Woodereeve from the pursuit of the ruthless Prior, than in the numerous apparitions of Sir Reginald de Folville, even though it is his spirit that slays Sir Gaston de Blondeville in open tourney and the Prior in his cell, and that convinces the King of Woodereeve's innocence as he was being led to execution on an accusation of witchcraft. Ghosts that do so much lose their ghostlike privileges of inspiring alarm.

Even for her own amusement, Mrs. Radcliffe wrote no more. What her works were—their wonderful beauties, which scarcely seem her own, so common has she made them, her glaring defects, which have been imitated even more largely than her beauties, and have vitiated public taste to our own day—we have endeavoured to show. And it is not merely by her works that Mrs. Radcliffe must be judged; it is by her power over the minds of her contemporaries and her successors. None of

those who have followed her in the regions of romance have escaped her influence. Critics, poets,
have felt it. To her Hazlitt acknowledged that
he owed his love of moonlit night, autumn leaves,
and decaying ruins. Strange power that could
thus rule, thus awaken fictitious tastes, likings, and
feelings. Even more remarkable is it to see how
Mrs. Radcliffe has given the tone to minds far
loftier than her own. Scattered through her wild
stories we find thoughts and feelings, noble though
sad, which voices more eloquent than hers took up
and clothed in the beauty of immortal verse.

When the young and ardent Blanche de Villefort,
leaving her convent, finds herself transferred to the
majesty and the splendour of the Pyrenees, and
appeals to her father to share her delight, when he
replies with the sad confession : " From my mind
the illusion which gave spirit to the colouring of
nature is fading fast," we are compelled to remember that noble strain of Wordsworth's in which he
acknowledges :

> " The things which I have seen
> I now can see no more ;
>   *   *   *   *   *
> And yet I know where'er I go,
> That there hath passed away a glory from the earth."

This is one of the features of Mrs. Radcliffe's writings; they were eminently suggestive, not to vulgar minds who only took up the false and the horrible in which she indulged, but to fine poetical natures like Byron's, Wordsworth's, Mrs. Hemans's, and many of their generation. They knew the value of a fine thought, of a poetic image, and by taking they knew, too, how to transform it, for poets are the marvellous alchemists of all times. In dross doomed to perish they see the grain of pure gold, and casting by the earth in which it lies buried, they make it live for evermore. Invention, the creative faculty as it is called, is not, after all, the poet's greatest gift. He invents little, but he has a wonderful capacity of receiving the feelings and thoughts of his own times, and of giving them his.

Of all who have written in prose—who attempted verse and failed in it—none have been more akin to the great brotherhood than Anne Radcliffe.

END OF VOL. I.

For EU product safety concerns, contact us at Calle de José Abascal, 56–1°,
28003 Madrid, Spain or eugpsr@cambridge.org.

www.ingramcontent.com/pod-product-compliance
Ingram Content Group UK Ltd.
Pitfield, Milton Keynes, MK11 3LW, UK
UKHW010350140625
459647UK00010B/974